TAKING CARE
of
MOTHER

An Age of Transition

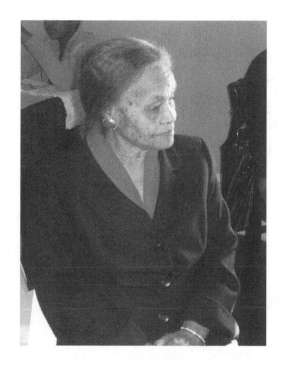

GWENDOLYN MCMILLAN LAWE

authorHOUSE®

AuthorHouse™
1663 Liberty Drive
Bloomington, IN 47403
www.authorhouse.com
Phone: 1 (800) 839-8640

Published by AuthorHouse 12/19/2017

ISBN: 978-1-5462-2079-4 (sc)
ISBN: 978-1-5462-2080-0 (hc)
ISBN: 978-1-5462-2078-7 (e)

Library of Congress Control Number: 2017918896

This book is dedicated to Mother, Modis Robinson McMillan, and to my husband, Theodore M. Lawe.

CONTENTS

PREFACE

Taking Care of Mother: An Age of Transition focuses on the changing family dynamics and the issues that evolve when a senior parent is no longer able to take care of the day-to-day activities of maintaining a household. It is difficult for all involved; however, it is especially hard when an individual notices frequent occurrences of forgetfulness, the inability to perform one's routine tasks, and repeated falls. These occurrences may not all happen at the same time. Often an individual will notice or the other people around will notice gradual changes. If the individual lives with someone—a spouse or an adult child—it might involve having someone assisting the elder person and actively observing the overall behavior. On the other hand, often the elderly person lives alone and is used to enjoying independency. If that is the case, someone in the family—preferably an adult child or spouse— needs to step in and become actively involved in the health care of the elderly family member.

Fortunately for me and for my mother, she lived in a neighborhood where she was surrounded by nieces, nephews, and friends. Therefore, even though I did not live in the same city, I felt somewhat comfortable that she was near family and friends and that they would watch after her. One niece in particular, Bonnie, was a nurse. She had worked in hospitals and nursing homes, and had taken care of her own invalid mother (my aunt) until her death. Bonnie was a caring individual and always checked on Mother and advised me of her needs—long before she had reached the stage of needing around-the-clock care. Bonnie encouraged me to begin paying more attention to Mother's health needs because, after all, she was getting older. She was already in her eighties although she seemed to be in relatively good health—both mentally and physically.

There are many levels of health care; and depending on the physical, mental, and financial circumstances of the individual, there are many services to assist families during this "age of transition." However, in the small town of Emory, Texas, where my mother lived, the services and facilities were limited. Because of this, I have compiled the information in this book based on my own experiences, so families may obtain the best possible care for their loved ones no matter where they live—particularly individuals who do not have the resources to totally finance this care.

ACKNOWLEDGMENTS

My mother, Modis Robinson McMillan, and the love of my life, Theodore Maxwell Lawe, taught me the true meaning of being a caregiver. I was inspired to write this book because taking care of Mother was a new experience for me, and I discovered there was a lot I needed to learn about resources for seniors—namely, home health-care agencies, specialty hospitals, and rehabilitation and nursing facilities. It was not until my mother's declining health that I became aware of the various divisions of health care and the need for good health-care professionals and facilities. As time passed and her health needs changed, I had to take an active role in seeing to it that she received the best care possible. Of course, I wanted her to stay at home in familiar surroundings as long as possible. During this time I learned that even though you want to allow your loved ones to be at home as long as possible, there comes a time when it is better for them to be in a facility where care is given around the clock.

Fortunately for me, when the time came for my mother to be admitted to a nursing facility, I was able to move her to a facility within a few minutes from where I lived. Up until that time, I was making weekly trips out of town to check on her. For one year, I visited with her daily. These were the most memorable days with my mother that I could have ever experienced.

Approximately seven months after my mother's death, I was faced with the unexpected illness and death of my husband. Thus, I dedicate this book to my mother and my husband.

INTRODUCTION

There are many individuals who helped me with this project—some knew and some were not aware. To the many people who work with the nonprofit organizations that provide assistance and resources to senior citizens, I am truly grateful. For it is through the efforts of these organizations that I received much of the information gained in my search for senior services, particularly those that are free to the public. Through watching infomercials on television, such as those advertising Medicare and Medicare Advantage plans, I was able to gather a lot of information, as well as going to their websites. My husband, Theodore M. Lawe, was always a great source of information and inspiration, and he was my best critic. At one time, my husband owned a home health-care business. I am truly grateful for his assistance in all of my projects. We were a team!

Finally, the most significant source of my inspiration for writing this book was my mother, Modis McMillan. It was because of her and our relationship during the past few years that I realized the need for individuals to know where to find resources for our loved ones through all of the transitioning stages of their later lives. I knew that I wanted her to have quality health care, and I knew that I was not equipped to give it to her. I had promised her that I would always take care of her or that I would see to it that someone else did if I could not. I would always be there for her, showing her the love and affection she had always shown to me, as well as to my three brothers. Equally important, I discovered that there were so many individuals like me who found some comfort in knowing they were not alone in learning how to meet the needs of their elderly parents. They needed guidance and encouragement. It is my hope that *Taking Care of Mother: An Age of Transition* will give some guidance to individuals who often do not plan for being a caregiver or the person responsible for the health-care needs of another individual—usually an elderly parent.

CHAPTER 1

A NEED FOR HELP

About five years ago, my mother expressed to me that she needed help with paying bills, as well as assistance with taking care of her financial affairs. Specifically, she said that she needed help with writing checks, balancing her accounts, and making sure that all bills, taxes, etc., were paid and current. Managing her finances overwhelmed her. She was always conscientious about paying her bills on time, but now she became nervous whenever she began writing the checks. With the exception of taxes, she had more than enough monthly income to cover her bills.

At this time, Mother was living alone and taking care of all of the day-to-day activities of maintaining her household. She still volunteered at the museum three or four days a week. She was involved with her church and was a member of the local genealogical society and the garden club, as well as several other organizations. She even served as the driver for some of her friends when they went out of town, particularly when visiting other churches or shopping in the surrounding communities. In other words, she kept a busy schedule. In spite of the fact that she was getting older, she seemed to be handling things quite well.

It was not until Mother had to be hospitalized for a low

potassium level that I became aware that more attention would be needed to monitor her health. The doctor informed us that she was experiencing some memory loss, which could have been a result of her low potassium and some other issues. Because she was hospitalized for four days, the hospital's social worker spoke with my brother Jewel (Chief) and me regarding my mother's care once she returned to her home. The social worker said that because Mother had Medicare, a doctor's referral would qualify her for having a home health nurse and aide visit her. The social worker gave me information about the services that would be offered, which also included the name of a home health agency. We decided that having this service would be a good idea. Within a few days after Mother returned home, a home health nurse began coming once a week, an aide came twice a week, and a physical therapist came on a different schedule. We were very pleased with this service. It gave me an added degree of comfort knowing that Mother would have someone checking on her on a regular basis. At first, because of her past independence, Mother had some reservations about someone assisting her, especially with her shower and personal care. However, after she had established a rapport with the home health workers, she too seemed to enjoy having someone come in and assist with her care.

I soon learned that the turnover rate for home health workers was high, and often when Mother got comfortable with an aide, she would no longer be assigned to her. Also, because most of the home health workers were young, there were instances when the nurses or aides would go on maternity leave. This meant that Mother had to adjust to a new person. After about two years, we began to have other problems that, in my opinion, interfered with the quality of Mother's care. For example, the aide who assisted her in getting out of bed, gave her showers, and helped with breakfast began coming later and later. She said it was because her patient load was growing. This continued until finally I decided that coming at 5:00 p.m. or later was too late to do the tasks that had been assigned and agreed upon (getting Mother out of bed, giving her a bath, dressing her, and assisting with her medications).

I felt that even though an aide's workload might have increased, it should not have meant moving Mother's schedule back from morning to evening. When I registered a complaint, another aide was assigned. That meant getting used to another person, and Mother's memory was already deteriorating. Fortunately, she seemed to adjust well. However, we started having problems again with the time that aides or nurses came and the number of visits per week. At first, we were informed that Medicare would not continue to pay for a nurse. The nurse told us that Medicare would only pay for an aide once a week instead of twice. Later, she told me that Medicare might stop paying for Mother's care all together. I decided it was time to see about using another agency (even though the rules for Medicare were supposed to be the same everywhere). We changed doctors and got a referral for another agency. Although the previous agency had limited the nurse's visits (all paid by Medicare), the new agency gave her more visits, as well as two days a week for an aide.

At this time, Mother decided that she didn't feel confident about taking care of any of her financial obligations, and she no longer wanted to drive. Although this was a very difficult time and many decisions had to be made regarding her finances, Mother and I had already done some planning as far as her financial affairs were concerned. My name was already on her checking, savings, and stock accounts. So this transition was somewhat simplified. My mother-in-law had been a victim of fraud when a stranger approached her and convinced her to take money out of her checking account and give to the stranger, even though she did not clearly understand why she needed to do so. I felt that we

3

were guarding against this kind of thing happening to my mother if I had the checkbooks, credit cards, etc.

Often when the time comes that a senior should no longer be driving, it creates a problem because the senior still feels able to drive and is not willing to surrender the keys to the car. So we were fortunate that my mother decided this on her own. She gave me the keys long before I expected and without my asking for them. Previously, when Mother was driving and working at the museum, she and her friends often went to the senior center for lunch. This was another program provided through the government to enable seniors to have hot meals daily and to socialize with other older adults in the community.

The center also offered programs that disseminated information regarding services provided to seniors living in the county. Most of the seniors were on Medicare, and many were on Medicaid as well. At the time, Mother was on Medicare, and she had a supplemental insurance policy. Because of her income, she did not qualify for some of the services, but there were many whose benefits she did enjoy. Many cities have senior centers. They serve as excellent places for seniors to spend time with other seniors. Some even provide transportation to and from the centers. Some cities also have adult day care centers for seniors who only need care during the day. In my mother's hometown, there was just one center. In larger cities, however, the city or county often offers these programs.

The same program that offered daily lunches at the senior center also offered a "Meal-a-Day" program that delivered meals to the individuals' homes. Once Mother was no longer driving, this was another plus for her care at home. Now, not only was someone coming by to check on her health, but someone else also checked on her daily when delivering the lunches. Because Mother did not eat much, often there was enough left over for a small meal in the evening. (I imagine that was the intent of having large servings.) Since the lunches were only delivered on weekdays, they brought extra food and snacks on Fridays so she would have something to eat on Saturday and Sunday as well.

When I visited Mother during the week, I often took her to the senior center so she could get together with her friends—even if she did not eat there. On some occasions, she and I both would have lunch at the center. Reservations were not required, so we did not have to plan ahead. When she felt like it, we would visit her sister or friends in the community, eat at restaurants, go to the museum, and even attend some of her civic meetings. Mother, as well as several other members of the museum's volunteer staff, enjoyed meeting at the senior center and at the museum for lunch and fellowship. We both enjoyed going out, even if it was just for a cup of coffee.

Although I visited Mother weekly, she needed daily help, so I hired someone to come in. At first, this seemed to be the perfect situation. They got along well, and Dijana fit right in with the family. In fact, she was a great worker and took pride in preparing meals for us whenever she knew that any family members would be visiting. My brother Chief was particularly fond of her cooking. Dijana knew that Mother loved sweets, and about once a week, she baked a cake. She served my mother ice cream (Mother's favorite) nightly. She assisted with the grocery shopping, cleaned, and usually did anything else that she felt was needed. Although she had a home, she treated Mother's home as her own. It was such a blessing to have found her.

Not long after beginning to work for my mother, Dijana took on several other jobs during the day. This often interfered with her having ample time to do Mother's work. However, she often checked on Mother during the day (which was not part of our agreement), so I tried to work with her. Mother seemed to be comfortable staying alone during the day because she knew that Dijana would check on her and often come and help her out, if needed, during her breaks from her other jobs. All Mother had to do was call. If necessary, Dijana could check on Mother around the clock, and she could be there in a matter of minutes. Since I lived over an hour away, Dijana's being near gave me an added degree of comfort.

Dijana worked for Mother for several months, and for the most part, we were satisfied with her work. We always tried to include her in family meals and celebrations. Then she became ill and no longer could work for Mother. We were very sorry to lose her as an employee, and we were concerned about her health. At that time, it was necessary to continue with the service of a home health agency, as well as find someone else to stay with Mother. Again I searched the newspaper for someone looking for employment who would be willing to stay with Mother at night. There was an advertisement in the local paper, but by the time I called, the person was no longer seeking employment.

My mother had a niece who had lost her home by fire and needed somewhere to stay. I decided to see if she would like to stay with Mother. I felt that this could be a win-win situation. Mother would have someone living with her, and her niece would have a place to live as well. As my mother's niece was only ten years younger than my mother, she was not able to do all of the work that Dijana had done, but because she spent most of her time at home, it gave Mother someone to be with her around the clock most of the time. They enjoyed watching television and had similar tastes in food (ice cream).

In March 2012, my younger brother, Jewel (Chief), passed away suddenly of an apparent heart attack. He was single and lived in another city. I am sure that, as a result, this was also one of the reasons that Mother's health seemed to decline. Chief had been the brother who had assisted me with Mother's care in the past, especially in the decision-making for her care. However, much to my surprise, Mother dealt with this life-changing event better than I had expected. Although I had to step up and take care of the funeral and other arrangements, I still wanted to include the rest of the family—my brothers Harold (the youngest) and Alfred (the oldest)—in making the plans. These types of events, in many cases, either bring a family closer or separate them. Thankfully, I think that it brought us closer. We all were able to give input into how things would be handled. Given Mother's health condition, I was the one (along with my husband and Harold) who had to make trips out of town to settle Chief's affairs, which included clearing out his home, moving his things, going to probate court, and preparing his home for sale. Fortunately, Harold, Ted, and I were able to take care of Chief's affairs in approximately one year, including the sale of his house.

While dealing with the death of one son, Mother was also dealing with the fact that her oldest son, Alfred, had been admitted to a VA nursing home facility. During this time, my mother's health seemed to decline even more rapidly, particularly her mental health. Maybe this was part of the grieving process over losing Chief—the one who was going to take care of her—and losing the daily contact that she'd had in the past with Alfred. Chief had been looking forward to selling his house and moving back to Emory so he could take care of her. He had already started staying for a week or so at a time when he visited her and often told her all of the things he was doing to his house in order to sell it. During that time, he tried to take care of the chores around Mother's house that Dijana could not do. He also made sure that her pantry was stocked with groceries and other household items before he went home. Mother really looked forward to those visits, and Chief enjoyed them as well. Although Chief had not lived in Emory since his sophomore year in college, he was happy to be near his best friend, Fred, again. Other than spending time with Fred, he hardly left the house while visiting Mother. If he wasn't with her, she would always say, "He's probably with Fred." Mother also enjoyed the fact that Fred visited her when Chief was there. He often brought her meals, even when Chief was not there. She lovingly referred to Fred as Chief's other brother. They were that close.

On Christmas Day, 2012, there was a sudden change in Mother's health. At first, I thought it might be temporary, but it was not. This was a traumatic experience for me because it was the first Christmas without Chief. There was snow on the ground, so Mother and I were spending the day at home with none of the other family members. This alone was hard. We had never spent Christmas without some family members. On Christmas Eve, we watched television and stayed up late, which we usually did when it was just the two of us. I even did some holiday cooking. As usual, I did most of the cooking while we discussed recipes. Mother usually gave some input on how to cook certain items, especially the dressing. Around midnight, when we decided to go to bed, Mother said, "I was just thinking about Chief." I told her that I was thinking of him too. Little did I know that this would be one of our last conversations that she initiated.

When I went in to give Mother her coffee on Christmas morning, she did not want it. She did not speak; she just refused the coffee. This was unusual because we always drank coffee, especially in the morning. Although she was a person of few words, we always had coffee and conversation the first thing in the morning. Later on, whenever I tried to sit her up to have coffee, she indicated that she was in severe pain. After a while, I decided to just let her rest. There wasn't much else I could do. Because it was Christmas Day and there was snow on the ground, I decided that I would not try to take her to the doctor for two reasons: (1)

I could not lift her and get her to the car, and (2) I was afraid to drive in the snow. Because of the snow, we spent the day alone. Neither of my brothers nor my daughter and grandkids wanted to attempt the drive.

On the day after Christmas, I called the paramedics first thing in the morning to take Mother to the hospital. She went in the ambulance, and I drove close behind. The snow was still on the ground, but I knew that I had to go with her. I tried to put my fear of driving in the snow aside. Mother's care was the priority. She spent several days in the hospital, and I stayed there with her. It was not the kind of holiday we had anticipated, but at least we were together.

When she returned home, it was evident that she would need twenty-four-hour care. Her niece had not gone to the hospital with us because she was spending Christmas with her sons. Her niece served as more of a companion than an actual caregiver. Because I had to have help immediately, I hired the only person I knew was available at the time. From December 2012 to November 2013 (almost a year), Mother had to have home health-care services as well as private-care individuals to look after her. Her niece still lived with her as well. Mother had been diagnosed with dementia when she was hospitalized, and it had advanced. She had become dependent on someone for everything. During those eleven months, she was under the care of three doctors. She needed assistance when walking, but I was still able to take her to the doctors' appointments. By staying in her home, I feel that Mother was happier than she would have been anywhere else. The care that she received was probably not the same quality that she could have gotten elsewhere (such as a nursing facility), but she was comfortable in her home. By this time, she had become totally lost when she visited me at my house, but she still seemed to function better in familiar surroundings—her home. Therefore, bringing her to Dallas to spend time with me was no longer an option. I had to spend more time with her in her home instead.

Because of Mother's health issues, and because now her private caregiver was occupying most of the living space in the house, my husband and I decided we should add on to her house so I would have a comfortable place to stay when I visited Mother and when both of us stayed with her. In order to involve Mother in the process, I let her select the carpet for my apartment, which was created by enclosing what had been Mother's carport. Also, because Mother was not able to go to the museum anymore, I needed to spend more time with her and start spending some time at the museum too. Mother had previously kept the museum open four days a week. Just as my mother's health had declined, the other museum volunteers also had suffered a decline in their health—three had passed away and the others were no longer able to maintain a weekly schedule. Therefore, in order for the museum to remain open and Mother to still spend time there, I began opening it when I was in town.

On two occasions, I took Mother to the clinic in Emory, although her primary doctors were located in Sulphur Springs, about twenty miles away. Because she had a pressure sore (decubitus ulcer) on her bottom, caused by sitting in her recliner all day, I felt that a doctor needed to treat it (although all he did was look at it). I really did not think that he examined it carefully, but he *was* the doctor. I had been told by the home health agency that Medicare would only allow a nurse's visit once a week, unless there were doctor's orders that she be seen more than that. So I requested an order from the doctor to have the nurse from the home health agency treat the wound at least twice a week instead of the aide. He said the wound did need to be treated by a nurse. My cousin Bonnie, who was a registered nurse (RN), also had told me that the wound needed to be treated by the nurse—not an aide. It was my understanding that a nurse was treating the wound, but the aide continued to do the treatments despite the doctor's orders. At least it was my assumption that the orders were given, although they were not followed.

Bonnie continued to check on Mother regularly and advise me of her condition, as well tell me what things I might need to purchase, such as a pillow for her to sit on while in her recliner and several other items needed to improve her care. In November, at Bonnie's suggestion, I took Mother to a wound center in nearby Sulphur Springs, the nearest one to Emory. Actually Bonnie and her husband took us. They were familiar with the wound center, and I was not. I had no idea that the wound had gotten so bad mainly because of the lack of proper treatment by the nurse (and the home health agency). Upon reflection, it is my belief that the doctor at the clinic, as well as the nurses and aides at the home health-care agency, was responsible for the eventual wound care that my mother needed. However, that is another matter altogether. The doctor at the wound center gave Mother a referral to Mesquite Specialty Hospital because it was near where I lived.

Within a few days, I drove to Emory and took Mother to Mesquite, where she was admitted to the hospital. I was allowed to stay in the room with her the entire time. I felt that to be in a new place would be too much of a shock for someone with memory problems. This experience was good for both of us—she saw a family member's face and heard a familiar voice. I was able to spend quality time with her as we learned how to live under these new circumstances. Little did I know that we would now have a new bond between us. I also learned that it was a privilege to be able to share the many hours we would now be sharing—getting to know each other from a totally different perspective. As her dementia progressed, Mother was no longer talking, except on rare occasions. Sometimes it was a simple "good morning" or a one-word answer to a question. I had to learn how to have conversations when only one of us was talking. I learned how precious it was to get a smile, a nod, or a simple answer to a question.

Mother remained at Mesquite Specialty Hospital for six weeks and was then placed in a center for rehabilitation that was also in Mesquite. She had excellent doctors who gave her the skilled treatment she needed. Fortunately for me, she was placed in a hospital and later in a rehabilitation facility near my home, and she was able to continue with the same doctor at both facilities, as well as skilled wound nurses.

Until Mother was in the Mesquite Specialty Hospital, I knew very little about her insurance, Medicare, and Medicaid (although she did not have Medicaid). Prior to this, she had been in the hospital a few times for brief stays, she had been taken to the hospital by ambulance a few times, and I had become the person responsible for getting her prescriptions from the pharmacy. Since most of these expenses were covered by her insurance and Medicare, I wrote the checks for the copayments, but I was not involved enough to know what Medicare would and would not pay. While she was in the hospital, I received a call from the medical supply company where she had gotten her hospital bed and wheelchair for her home. When she received these items, we paid a copayment and Medicare paid the remainder (which was for rent, not purchase). Therefore, while she was in the hospital, Medicare would not continue to pay for her bed and wheelchair if they were not being used. In other words, they would not pay for the use of two beds when she was using only one of them. At this time, I thought these items were hers; I was wrong. There is a rule that Medicare will rent the medical equipment for a period of time, and at the end of that time, the equipment becomes the property of the patient. Rather than have the medical supply company come and pick up the equipment, I decided to pay the balance so Mother would own her bed and wheelchair if she ever needed them again. I felt that if she returned home, we would not have to go through Medicare to rent the equipment again and pay an additional copay. I also thought that since my husband, my brothers, and I were all senior citizens, we might need the equipment for ourselves. Because the equipment had been rented for almost a year, the balance owed was minimal.

While Mother was in the hospital, the hospital social worker explained to me that Medicare would pay Mother's hospital and rehabilitation bill. Once released from the hospital, Medicare would cover up to one hundred days of rehabilitation. Because by now I realized that Mother would not be returning home once she finished rehabilitation, I needed to determine where she would go. After talking with my brother Harold, we decided it would be better for Mother to stay at the same facility and move into the nursing home there. When the one hundred days expired, we wanted to already know where Mother would be moving (and how it would be funded).

During this time, we also started to look into the cost of rehabilitation (if Medicare was not paying for it) and the cost of residing in a nursing home (which Medicare does not pay). In doing my research on the cost of nursing home care, I realized that Mother could pay for it for only a short period. However, since one does not know the life expectancy of an individual placed in a long-term facility, she would eventually be out of money and unable to pay for her care. Therefore, it was time to look at Medicaid, which covers approximately 80 percent of a resident's fees for nursing home care, according to my research. (This is what the finance office at the rehabilitation center told me.) Medicaid also will pay for the entire cost of nursing home care if the patient's income is below a certain level.

I decided that it was time to seek professional assistance to see how Mother could qualify for Medicaid, although her income, savings, and property would not allow her to qualify. When seeking help from nonprofessionals, I found that the first word of advice was: "She'll lose her house." Although my mother's care was far more important than property, I decided that hiring a law firm to help her qualify for Medicaid was the next step. There are too many steps involved, and because this involves doing business with the federal government, it is advisable to get help from someone who understands Medicaid and understands the law. We did, and we were pleased with the results—she qualified for Medicaid to assist in funding her stay in the nursing home. Although Mother was in the nursing home while the Medicaid application was still pending, Medicaid paid half and she paid half until it was approved. Because my mother's home was no longer in her name, there was no danger in our losing our homeplace. With the assistance of a law firm, it only took a few months for Mother to qualify for Medicaid. However, if the Medicaid had not been approved, she would have had to reimburse it for those months while waiting for approval (approximately $11,000).

In April, while Mother was still in rehabilitation, she was rushed to the ER at a nearby hospital because her blood sugar was high. That's when we learned she was now a diabetic (at age eighty-eight). I asked the physician if that was common to become a diabetic so late in life, and he said it was not uncommon. I moved into the hospital with her just as I had done before. After approximately five more weeks in the hospital, she was once again returned to rehabilitation at the same facility. She had to be readmitted just as though she was a new patient (for rehabilitation). While in the hospital, the rehab center had packed up her things and asked me to come and get them. You see, Medicare would not pay for her hospital room and her room in rehabilitation at the same time (just as it wouldn't pay for the hospital bed at home when she was in the hospital previously). Upon her return to rehabilitation, I learned that she had forty-five days of Medicare left, and after that she would be released to the nursing home. (I had already decided that she should remain in the same facility.) The move from rehabilitation to a skilled nursing facility would only require her to move to another wing. She would continue having the same doctors and therapists, and in some cases, she would have the same caregivers for feeding and grooming. After visiting several other facilities, I saw no real advantage in moving to another facility. It would have meant starting over in many ways.

On June 4, Mother was rushed to the hospital due to an extreme drop in her blood sugar level. She stayed overnight and returned to the nursing home the next day. According to her doctor at the hospital, who was not her regular doctor, it is more critical when the blood sugar is low than when it is high. He told me that insulin can be given when it is high, and it will be lowered. But when it is low, it is more dangerous. I was glad that they were able to stabilize her blood sugar and get her back to the nursing home the next day. Mother remained at the same facility with the same doctors from the time she was admitted in April.

Because I was retired and Mother was only fifteen minutes from my home, I spent my afternoons with her. Once I adjusted to this stage of transition, there were so many things that became enjoyable. Little things, like having a cup of coffee together, became big things. And if it was a good day, we had coffee and cookies! Actually I learned that every day that God allowed us to spend together was a good day, and some were better. However, I also learned to accept the days when I visited and she slept the entire time—only waking up to be fed—as good days too. She was there!

CHAPTER 2

EVALUATING AND DETERMINING THE KIND OF CARE NEEDED

While the elderly person is still in charge of his or her mental capacities, it is advisable that someone, such as an adult child or a spouse, begin identifying and locating all of the accounts (checking, savings, etc.), insurance policies, property deeds, stock information, etc. If all of this information is not readily available, much of it can be obtained by carefully examining the mail and bank statements. At this time, it is also a good idea to have another family member's name added to all accounts. Fortunately, my mother had the foresight to add my name to all of her accounts. She also had a will. If documents such as a will and a power of attorney have not been prepared, this is the time to do so. This is also a good time to seek the services of an attorney to make sure that all legal documents are in order. It might also be advisable to use a financial advisor if there are several accounts, large amounts of money, and stocks and bonds.

Along with the aforementioned information, I made copies of all medications and a list of doctors, along with a list of upcoming appointments when I started assisting with Mother's care. I recommend doing this as one of the initial steps when becoming a caregiver. If the elderly person has been going to a doctor alone, it might be good to start monitoring all appointments, medical procedures, vaccinations, etc. Also, if the elderly person is ever hospitalized, speak with the hospital social worker regarding services available after the release from the hospital. Ask about the "three midnight rule," which applies when Medicare provides Skilled Nursing Facility (SNF) care following hospitalization. It is recommended that caregivers review the *Medicare Benefit Policy Manual* to answer more specific questions that one might have. This is also a good time to begin collecting information on senior issues for your own library—books, magazines, newspapers, articles, brochures, etc. If you are over fifty, I also suggest that you join AARP and get an early start on learning about senior issues.

When I started going to doctors' appointments with my mother, each physician was helpful in advising me on the steps I needed to take in managing her care. Once you have taken on the responsibility of overseeing the health care of your senior family member—and you have decided that you need to assist in the day-to-day care of the individual—it is necessary to evaluate what your senior can and cannot do. You can do this by making a checklist similar to the one below. These are the kinds of questions that a potential caregiver or home health-care agency will ask.

Kinds of Care Needed
Checklist

o Dressing
o Showering/bathing
o Medication assistance
o Preparing meals

o   Feeding
o   Incontinence (care/supplies)
o   Is there memory loss?
o   Can the individual assist?
o   Does the individual use a wheelchair or walker?

Based on the information that you receive from the individual and the doctors, does the individual have any of the health issues listed below? The kinds and levels of care needed for your senior relative will be determined in many cases by the health issues of the individual. You should also have a list of the current medications, both prescribed and over the counter. This is also the kind of information needed if you go to a doctor's appointment with the senior, particularly if it is a new doctor.

Current Health of the Elderly Person Checklist

o   Alzheimer's/dementia
o   Cancer
o   High or low blood pressure
o   Heart disease
o   Diabetes
o   Arthritis
o   Hearing loss
o   Vision problems
o   Dental problems/dentures
o   Respiratory, use of oxygen
o   Wandering
o   Falling
o   Other

Just as it is important to evaluate the health status of your family member, it is also wise to make a checklist to begin locating all of the necessary documents you will need for continuing to offer your family member the best care at home, in the hospital, or in a rehabilitation or nursing facility. In my mother's case, she had most of her important documents stored in drawers in her bedroom. I had to look for the documents and then make a list of those I had located. If the documents cannot be located, examining all incoming mail will usually provide valuable information about checking, investments, insurance, etc. I have included below a checklist of documents that should be located. Making a checklist and including such things as account numbers will prove to be most beneficial in taking care of financial matters.

Financial and Other Materials to Be Located Checklist

- o Bank statements
- o Checks and checkbooks
- o Driver's license
- o Identification cards
- o Membership cards
- o Credit cards
- o Documentation for all financial accounts
- o Insurance policies

By monitoring the mail, much of this information can be obtained. (It is a good idea to have mail forwarded.)

Recognizing Dementia. Dementia is a broad term to describe many brain diseases. The most common form of dementia is Alzheimer's disease (60 to 80 percent, according to the Alzheimer's Association). Dementia becomes more common as a person ages. Only 3 percent of people between ages sixty-five and seventy-four have dementia; but 47 percent of people over eighty-five have some form of dementia. Therefore, the longer people live, the greater the chance of developing dementia, which affects the brain's ability to think, reason, and remember. Because dementia progresses slowly, by the time it is diagnosed (or by the time that a family member observes it in his or her loved one), the process has been taking place for a long time. An individual may experience more than one kind of dementia. Although there is no cure, it is important for the caregiver to become educated about the disease as much as possible.

Here are some of the symptoms/signs of dementia:

- Depression and/or anxiety
- Agitation
- Problems with balance
- Tremors
- Speech or language difficulty
- Trouble eating or swallowing
- Delusions or hallucinations
- Memory distortions
- Wandering or restlessness[1]

Although these are common signs, this does not mean that your loved one will exhibit all of them. The most recognizable sign (as I observed with my mother) was memory loss. When I took her to the doctor for her regular appointments, the doctor would ask such questions as these: What is your name? How old are you? Do you know what day this is? Where are we? When I noticed how she struggled to answer these simple questions, it made me aware that

---

[1] . "Dementia," wikipedia.org/wiki/Dementia (accessed October 17, 2014).

she had much more memory loss than I had suspected. I had never thought to ask such questions. I noticed that there were things she did not remember, but she still seemed alert, and we still had long talks, cooked together, and enjoyed each other. To the best of my knowledge, it was at this point that she was given medications to aid her memory. I don't know if any brain scans or tests were ever administered to determine her condition. Since she was over eighty-five, I presumed that because she was unable to answer such basic questions with ease, she had dementia or Alzheimer's disease (although no neurological tests were ever given). Therefore I began reading about this condition and attending workshops for caregivers and family members of patients with dementia or Alzheimer's disease. Often local chapters of the Alzheimer's Association will offer seminars or provide speakers for programs to disseminate information about these conditions. On several occasions, I was able to hear speakers at regular meetings of a few of the organizations I belong to and also at my church during its "Senior Saints" programs. Although I don't know if her treatments would have been any different or the results any more successful, I think I should have inquired about having neurological tests done when I was first told that my mother was suffering from dementia. Because there is no cure for dementia, Mother's doctor explained to me that her memory medication might slow down memory loss, but it would not cure the dementia.

One of my aunts lived for over ten years with Alzheimer's disease. I can remember when family members first began to notice some of her symptoms. On one occasion, I remember her telling about a time when she was driving home, and for a moment, she was totally lost. On other occasions when I visited with her, she was always organizing her papers. She had been a busy person; she worked for a nonprofit organization and was very involved in her church and other civic organizations. Several times neighbors would find her walking or roaming in the neighborhood. She would be disoriented and would need to be taken home. Eventually she became bedridden and required around-the-clock care.

My mother had been around her sister (my aunt), as well as several other relatives and neighbors who were experiencing various degrees of dementia. One of the things I observed that was common with all of them is that they would repeatedly ask the same questions. At the museum where my mother and several other seniors worked as volunteers, the average age was around eighty. My mother and one of the other ladies made an agreement that they would watch each other for signs of dementia. They worked together for several years after the agreement until the other lady had to stop volunteering. It was apparent that she was having some issues with her memory. She had home health care for a while and was later admitted to a nursing home, where Mother and I visited her. Although she had dementia, she was always glad to see us, and we were glad to see her as well. As time passed I still visited her, but my mother was not able to do so.

My mother always was a sweet, quiet, loving person. As her dementia progressed, I noticed that she became very disoriented when she was in unfamiliar places, and then in her own home. Her conversations became more and more limited to responding to questions rather than generating or initiating the conversation. Unlike what I had read, Mother's appetite remained good, but she ate slower. She became fascinated with folding; whether it was a blanket, a towel, or a piece of paper, she was always folding. She seldom became noticeably irritated or agitated. On one occasion, she took a walk in the neighborhood, and some of her young nieces, who also lived in the neighborhood, walked back home with her. This is the only time that I know of that she actually left home alone. For the most part, she continued to have the same gentle spirit that she'd always had.

I learned that making statements to her was the best way to communicate as she began losing her memory. Questions had to be simple, such as "How are you?" This would not require Mother to search for an answer for a long period. She stared into space sometimes, but on those rare occasions, that beautiful smile was still visible. Her speech became mostly limited to a nod of the head, a simple uh-huh, and rarely a brief statement, such as "good morning." It seemed that because of her mind, her body appeared to stop functioning so she needed everything done for her, which happens with Alzheimer's disease. She had to be cared for around the clock. Because I had several friends whose parents were suffering from some form of dementia, we often compared our parents' behavior. Although there were some commonalities, symptoms and behaviors were very different.

My mother never had any type of heart problems or strokes (of which I was aware). However, if you are responsible for the care of an elderly person, there are some warning signs of which you should be aware. Dementia does not mean that your loved one will have congestive heart failure or a stroke, but when you become a caregiver of an elderly person, it is important that you learn as much as possible about such conditions. My mother did not have heart problems initially, but eventually she did. Her doctor advised me that as an individual ages, all organs begin to suffer various kinds of failure. Some of these conditions include congestive heart failure, heart attack, and stroke.

Warning Signs of Congestive Heart Failure

Congestive heart failure means that the heart does not pump as strongly as it should. Therefore, the blood that is normally pumped forward backs up into the lungs and other parts of the body. This does not mean that the heart has stopped. Some of the signs for congestive heart failure include the following:

- Three- to five-pound weight gain in one week
- Swelling in the ankles
- Waking up at night short of breath and needing to sit up to catch one's breath
- Unusual shortness of breath
- Coughing
- More fatigue than usual

The doctor should be informed about these warning signs.

Warning Signs of a Heart Attack

A heart attack happens when a blood vessel (artery) in your heart is completely blocked, usually by a blood clot. A part of the heart muscle no longer receives a blood supply, and this causes some portion of the heart muscle to die. Warning signs include the following:

- Pain may occur when resting and does not subside with rest.
- A feeling of severe, sudden chest pain that resembles heavy pressure, squeezing, or fullness occurs. It is sometimes described as feeling like "a belt pulled tight around my chest" or "an elephant standing on my chest."
- Pains may be accompanied by sweating, dizziness, vomiting, nausea, indigestion, a bloated feeling, paleness, weakness, anxiety, and difficulty breathing.
- Pain may spread to the shoulders, down one or both arms, neck, back, teeth, jaws, or ear lobes.

Some medications that may be taken while having a heart attack are aspirin, a beta-blocker, or an ACE inhibitor.

If the patient has these warning signs, call 911 immediately and go to the hospital.

Warning Signs of a Stroke

Just as a heart attack is due to a blockage in your heart, a stroke is blockage in or a disturbance in blood supply to a part of the brain. The warning signs depend upon the part of the brain that is involved. Warning signs include the following:

- Weakness or paralysis on one side of the body
- Problems with speech and language
- Poor balance
- Not knowing what happens on one side of the body
- Trouble swallowing
- Problems with bladder or bowel control
- Problems with memory, thinking, or problem solving
- Poor vision, loss of vision on one side, or double vision
- Numbness
- Problems getting around and caring for oneself.[2]

Elderly Person's Financial Status Checklist

o Insurance/Medicare/Medicaid
o Life insurance
o Money in the bank or investments
  o Savings
  o Checking
  o Stocks/bonds

---

[2] . *Patient Information Guide*, Dallas Regional Medical Center, 29–31.

o Real estate
   o Own Home _____ Rent_____
   o Rental or other property
o Income:
   o Retirement
   o Social Security
   o Annuities
o Expenses:
   o Rent/mortgage
   o Utilities
   o Phone
   o Electricity
   o Cable or dish
   o Credit (retail)
   o Lawn care
   o Property taxes
   o Other

CHAPTER *3*

AN END TO INDEPENDENT LIVING

Once it is determined that you or your loved one can no longer live independently at home, it is time to begin looking at various kinds of housing and the many levels of care provided by each. While my mother was in the hospital, before being released to a rehabilitation facility, I began researching facilities that would meet her needs. At the same time, I became more interested in getting information about levels of care because, at some point in time, this information might be beneficial to me (for me), my spouse, or other family members. Sometimes we become caregivers when it is not in our plan. Therefore, no preparation has been made.

In this chapter, I share what I have learned about the different kinds of housing and the kinds of care provided by each. As I am not a health-care professional, I basically use layman's terms to describe the resources and services that I found available for my mother.

When I began doing my research, I considered the facilities and services that were in or near my mother's home in Emory, Texas. As this is a very small town in eastern Texas, facilities and services were very limited. I used a website, Senior Advisor, which allowed me to browse over 105,000 senior communities in Texas for pricing, ratings, and reviews. In the Emory area, there were only twelve, and of those only three were SNF (skilled nursing facilities). On the other hand, there were 625 in Dallas, but only 72 were SNFs.[3]

There are many other websites that might assist you in your search for senior services. I have listed twenty such websites in Appendix A that I found very informative. Many Internet sites indicate that they offer "free" services, such as supplying locations of facilities, etc.; however, these sites offer ads for various services or equipment that seniors may need. To get the free information regarding nursing homes, you are asked to fill out a form with personal information only to get a message that you will be contacted later by phone. The websites that I have listed are sites that actually *are* free and have many informational resources for seniors. Some are organized and operated by government agencies or nonprofit agencies. Additionally, there are some organizations for seniors, i.e., AARP, where membership includes publications that give valuable information on topics of interest to seniors. In my opinion, it is still better to visit the facilities in person, if possible.

Assisted Living (at home or apartment)

There are times when an individual might need some form of assisted living. Among those are various kinds of multigenerational housing. If a senior family member is in relatively good health and needs minimal assistance, in some cases it might be advisable for

---

[3] . "Nursing Homes," www.senioradvisor.com/ind/nursing-home (accessed June 16, 2017).

the senior to move in with his or her children and/or grandchildren for assistance.

An assisted living facility is housing for the elderly or individuals with disabilities. This type of housing is excellent for individuals who value their independence but still need some assistance in day-to-day activities to maintain healthy living, i.e., meal preparation, house cleaning, etc. Some assisted living facilities also offer memory care services.

Home health-care providers are often used when an individual is able to stay at home with the assistance of a home health agency. These agencies provide various services that are paid by Medicare, with a referral from a doctor. These are some of the services provided by home health agencies:

o   Aides
o   Nurses
o   Therapists
o   Social workers

Private care providers are often used because many services cannot be provided through Medicare, and individuals may prefer to obtain these services on their own. Some of these services might be needed even though Medicare may not cover them:

o   Aides
o   Sitters
o   Homemakers/housekeepers
o   Personal shoppers

Specialty hospitals are long-term acute care (LTAC) facilities. Although most hospital stays are relatively brief, sometimes it is necessary for the elderly person to receive the services of a specialty hospital, i.e., for wound care, cancer, etc., instead of a general hospital. This care is usually covered through Medicare.

Rehabilitation centers are often required when an individual is released from the hospital and the next line of treatment is rehabilitation, which Medicare also covers as long as the doctor treating the patient makes the referral. Rehabilitation stays may be short term or long term. Rehabilitation centers are designed to assist in the recovery from an injury or an illness. They offer various services, such as physical therapy, occupational therapy, and speech therapy, to name a few. There are also rehabilitation centers for drug addiction and alcoholic addiction. However, these are not the kind of rehabilitation centers that would be beneficial for the type of seniors I am writing about.

Nursing homes are recommended when it is determined that the patient will not be able to return home after receiving treatment in a hospital or a rehabilitation center. Nursing homes provide the following:

- Skilled nursing, a term that Medicare uses to describe nursing care in a skilled nursing facility (SNF)—a nursing home
- Therapists (occupational, physical, speech, etc.)
- Transportation
- Doctors

We might feel that a nursing home is the next step, but there are certain things that will have to happen before admission to a nursing home. It takes some advanced planning to gain admittance.

Criteria for Nursing Home Admittance

First, there has to be a doctor's order for the patient to be admitted to a nursing home. Other criteria for evaluation will be needed to determine if moving to a nursing home will meet a "medical necessity"—for instance, if there is no way for the patient to be properly cared for at home and he or she needs to be taken care of around the clock. Some of the important considerations are these:

- Does the senior need assistance in taking medications?
- Is the senior suffering from dementia or Alzheimer's disease?
- Are there incidences of frequent falling?
- Are there frequent incidences of wandering?
- Is the senior in a wheelchair or confined to the bed?"

These are just some of the questions that must be answered in determining "medical necessity."

In visiting several nursing homes in the same geographical locations, I found that the cost of care varies. It is wise to visit several facilities and, if possible, gather information from friends who may have firsthand knowledge about specific locations. The Internet can also serve as a valuable resource. If you have narrowed your search to two or three facilities, I suggest that you visit them several times and at several times of day. That will enable you to see the residents in several settings because there are various activities going on throughout the day. It is especially a good idea to visit during mealtime to observe the cafeteria, the food, and the manner in which the residents are fed. I suggest you get a copy of the monthly calendar of activities for the residents. The calendar will show such activities as bingo, cards, dominoes, movie night, field trips, and parties for special occasions. Incidentally, in the hospital people are referred to as "patients," but in the nursing home they are "residents." That makes sense to me because that is where they live.

There are instances when active adults choose to move to retirement communities that offer independent as well as assisted living. **Active adult communities,** also known as continuing care retirement communities (CCRCs), are communities that allow the resident to enjoy independent living, and in some cases, they also offer assisted living as the need for health care changes. These communities tend to be more costly, and because they are not medical facilities, the resident must pay for them—not Medicare, Medicaid, or insurance. These communities provide excellent opportunities for seniors who are still able to live independently. They are not recommended if the senior is not in good health.

Hospice care is often the next step when a patient reaches advanced stages of a terminal illness. The patient is allowed to end life at home. Support services are given to the patient as well as to the family. Hospice care is covered under Medicare Part A. Information regarding hospice care benefits is available by visiting the Centers for Medicare and Medicaid Services website.

Doctors in the hospital or nursing home often will recommend hospice care. This care may be provided to the patient at home or in the nursing facility. Usually, there are professional staff members who will provide additional information if hospice care is an option. The same thing is true with palliative care. The physician should be able to describe the specific care for your loved one if hospice care is recommended.

Palliative care is care that relieves pain, symptoms, and stress caused by serious illnesses, improving patients' quality of life. Any health-care provider can give this care, and some specialize in it. The goal is to help patients with serious illnesses feel better. As with hospice care, one does not need to give up his or her doctor or treatments to receive palliative care.

CHAPTER 4

ADVANCED CARE PLANNING

Once an individual has experienced taking care of a loved one, whether it is a spouse, a parent, or oneself, there are so many lessons learned. Therefore, I would like to share some of the things I learned that enable me to give advice on what to expect when taking care of a loved one and how to avoid some of the challenges I had to deal with because I did not know what to expect. There are some things we can do for ourselves that will enable others to know how we want to be taken care of if/when the time comes. Some decisions I made for my mother, but many of the decisions that I made for her were based on discussions we'd had when she was mentally and physically able to give me some directives regarding her wishes. Because I was caring for her, I was better able to plan for my future if someone has to care for me. Also, it is important to know that if you are responsible for providing someone's care, you should also have a plan for someone else to take care of your loved one if you should die first. Just because you are the youngest does not mean that you will live longer. This should be indicated in a will.

Advanced care planning means planning ahead for how one wants to be treated if he or she becomes very ill or near death.

Sometimes people become very ill and are not able to let family members know their wishes. In Texas, the law allows the patient to tell the doctor how he or she wants to be treated through an advance directive. The patient is able to fill out forms stating how medical decisions should be carried out. If you are the caregiver, it is important to know if the patient has named an individual as the agent. I was named my mother's agent.

Some of the documents that are needed at this time are a *living will* (which tells family members and doctors what an individual does and does not want done), and a *medical power of attorney* (which enables an individual to name an agent). It is always important to let family know one's wishes before something happens. Mother had a will and a power of attorney. However, she did not have a living will or a medical power of attorney. After attaining the services of a law firm, she had them.

Because I have seen instances where the caregiver preceded the patient in death, it is important that you, as a caregiver, consider taking time to prepare now for a disability or a death to make it easier on your loved ones if someone should have to care for you. First, it is important to begin some kind of savings or investment plan. It is suggested that one set aside at least three to six months of living expenses to get through a difficult period without taking out a loan. Having a small amount of money taken automatically from one's paycheck and placed into a savings account is a great way to start preparing for an emergency. Also, it is worthwhile to keep a list of accounts and important documents so a relative (spouse, adult child, or other trusted person) can easily locate them. Because you do not want this information to fall into the wrong hands, keep it in a secure place where only you and selected others have access.

To determine whether you have an adequate amount of life and disability insurance, it might be wise to meet with your insurance agent. You might also want to consider long-term care insurance. Upon death, debts should be paid from your estate; however, there might be some exceptions. Be clear that the individuals whom you want to have access to your accounts are named on the accounts. You can do this by having joint accounts with a spouse or a loved one so the individual has equal access to your account. You might prefer setting up an account that is payable on death (POD). A POD account only allows the person named to access the account after you die. To learn more about preparing your finances for a disability or death, visit www.mymoney.gov.[4]

Planning for a loved one's death. It is important to plan for death just as it is important to plan for living. Unfortunately, sometimes the death of a loved one comes as a total shock to the caregiver or the person responsible for the care of a loved one. Often little or no plans have been made for the final event—death. Therefore, if the individual responsible for the elderly person has not made any final plans, it is important to start now.

Once the elderly person has died, there are some immediate things that must be done. If you are the responsible party, you must first notify the funeral home that will be handling the services. The funeral home will make the arrangements to have the body picked up from home, the hospital, or the nursing home. After all family members have been contacted, one of the next things that should be done immediately is to notify the banks and other financial institutions so they can prevent an unauthorized person from withdrawing funds from the accounts. Stop payment on all automatic withdrawals from bank accounts and/or credit cards. Because stopping payments on all automatic withdrawals might be difficult, it is usually easier to just close any existing checking accounts. Although it is extremely important to be on the alert

---

[4] . "Preparing Financially for a Disability or Death," *Seniorific News*, October 2014, 20.

for individuals taking advantage of seniors, these practices are also equally prevalent in death. Thus, it is important to take preventive measures to ensure that banking and credit card accounts are not used after the loved one dies. Also inform the issuers of the credit cards to cancel the accounts. The Social Security Administration at www.ssa. gov/agency/contact should be contacted immediately, as well as any other provider of a pension or other payments to the deceased person. Locate all of the important documents and secure the deceased person's driver's license and Social Security card. (Remember that the Medicare card includes the Social Security number on it.) You will need several copies of the death certificate in order to take care of the deceased person's financial affairs.[5] Based on the number of accounts, initially it might be feasible to get from eight to ten copies of the certificate. In transacting business on behalf of the deceased person, you will often be asked to supply an original copy of the death certificate as well as a copy of your power of attorney.

It is very important to check the mail carefully for at least a year. Often bank accounts, credit accounts, and insurance policies will send statements after the individual's death. These may or may not be among those of which you are aware. Be careful that you are on the lookout for fraudulent creditors at this time as well.

If funeral arrangements have not been made through a prepaid funeral plan, compare several funeral homes before making a decision if time permits. There are many plans, and the costs vary. Have all insurance policies available. If the policy or policies will completely cover the funeral costs, the funeral home will probably take the responsibility of filing the claim. Include other family members, if possible, in the plans for the final arrangements. The funeral home personnel will also assist with the planning of the funeral, memorial, burial, or other services that you might require.

---

[5] . "Managing a Loved One's Finances after a Serious Life Event," *Seniorific News*, October 2014, 9.

CHAPTER *5*

INSURANCE, MEDICARE, AND MEDICAID

As we age and our health issues change, it is important to understand what medical coverage we have and exactly what each one covers. Likewise, if we are the primary caregivers for a loved one, we should have this information readily available for that individual as well.

If you have an insurance policy, you should review it to be sure of the extent of the coverage. Medicare covers most seniors as well. On the other hand, Medicaid is a totally different program with different requirements, which I have explained briefly.

Medicare

Medicare is a national health insurance program administered by the federal government. The program is for people ages sixty-five and older, although there are certain circumstances that allow younger individuals to qualify. Individuals with Medicare (or their family members or caregivers) should visit the official US Government website at www.medicare.gov to obtain the latest

Medicare information as well as information on supplemental insurance, sometimes called a Medigap policy.

There are four basic forms of Medicare coverage:

- Part A: Pays hospitalization costs
- Part B: Pays for physician services, lab and X-ray services, durable medical equipment, and outpatient and other services
- Part C: Medicare Advantage Plan (like an HMO or PPO), or Medigap, which is offered by private companies approved by Medicare
- Part D: Assists with the cost of prescription drugs

To be able to use Medicare Part A (for rehabilitation services), one must be hospitalized at least three consecutive days, be admitted to a Medicare-certified facility (often referred to as an SNF unit) within thirty days of discharge from a hospital or long-term care facility, and require further care for the same condition treated in the hospital. A physician must certify the need for daily skilled care, and the patient must not have exceeded the number of Medicare days within the benefit period. Medicare will pay 100 percent of approved services for the first twenty days of rehabilitation stay. After the twenty days and up to one hundred days, the individual is responsible for a copayment, which Medicare sets yearly, unless the individual has been approved for or has applied for Medicaid. Medicaid qualification varies from state to state. In Texas, if you are a single head of household, your income cannot be above $2,000 a month to qualify for Medicaid. That was what I was told when Mother was admitted to the nursing home. Although her income was above that requirement, it was still not high enough to afford living in a nursing home for a long period of time.

In a rehabilitation facility, Medicare Part A will cover room and board, all meals, labs and X-rays, nursing care, pharmacy, medical supplies and special equipment, oxygen, and various kinds of therapy.

Part B is voluntary, and one must pay an annual deductible as well as monthly premiums. Part B covers medical supplies and special equipment, various therapies, and enteral nutrition (sometimes called "tubal feeding") supplies.

Part C covers up to 80 percent of all covered supplies and services. The individual is responsible for the remaining 20 percent. Part C Medicare (Medigap) is supplemental health insurance coverage. "Medicare Part C is not a separate Medicare benefit. Part C is the part of the US Medicare policy that permits medical companies to offer supplemental Medicare benefits. These Medicare private health plans, such as HMOs and PPOs are known as a Medicare Advantage Plan."[6]

Part D, the Medicare prescription drug benefit, has evolved over the past nine years (since 2006) because of changes in the private plan marketplace, which changes every year, and the laws that regulate the program. Enrollees in these plans may experience changes in cost of premiums, which drugs are covered, and which pharmacies they can use.

UnitedHealthcare, Humana, and CVS Caremark have enrolled half of all participants in Part D. This level of market concentration has not changed much since 2006. UnitedHealthcare and Humana have held the largest shares of enrollment, but enrollment in CVS Caremark has grown through its acquisitions of other plan

[6] . "What Are Medicare Advantage Plans?" www.medicareadvantage.com (accessed June 16, 2017).

sponsors. However, UnitedHealthcare has maintained the lead throughout the nine years of the program.[7]

Because of the changes in the cost and coverage for Medicare Part D, it is wise to evaluate the plan annually. I would suggest using www.medicare.gov to compare plans and to answer all Medicare questions. Some local senior centers offer workshops and assistance in applying for Medicare. These services are provided at no cost.

Medicaid

Many seniors (age sixty-five and older) qualify for Medicaid and Medicare. Medicaid covers some services beyond those provided under Medicare, including nursing facility care beyond the one-hundred-day limit or skilled nursing facilities care that Medicare covers. Services that both agencies cover are paid by Medicare first; then Medicaid will pay the difference up to the state's payment limit. Because these payment limits vary from state to state, it is important that you do research for your specific state.

There is currently no federal provision for health coverage for adults without dependent children. However, if the individual is sixty-five or older (the age group we are considering), he or she may qualify for Medicaid coverage. Many states provide some coverage through federal waivers or state-funded programs for low-income individuals who do not qualify for Medicaid. Again, since these federal waivers and state-funded programs vary from state to state, it is important to find out what your state provides. Since many seniors who are on Medicare are not able to pay for nursing home care, it is necessary to apply for Medicaid to assist with the

---

[7] . Jack Hoadley, Laura Summer, Elizabeth Hargrave, Juliette Cubanski, and Tricia Newman, "Medicare Prescription Drug Benefit: What's Changed in 9 Years?" *Seniorific News,* October 2014.

payments. In this case, I recommend the services of an attorney to assist with applying for Medicaid. However, if you think that you qualify for Medicaid (and have not applied), the business officer at the nursing home often can assist with your eligibility by securing information pertaining to your income, assets, expenses, etc. The business officer will be able to tell you if you need the services of an attorney in order to process the application. The less assets (such as home, real estate, insurance cash value, and money in the bank) and income the individual has, the greater the chances for qualifying for Medicaid. Often an individual's income is too high to qualify for Medicaid, but the cost of nursing home care is still much greater than the income. Then it is necessary to apply for Medicaid in order to receive the needed care.

Because many seniors are veterans and receive most or all of their health care from the Veterans Administration (VA), many have no other source of health care except Medicare. In some cases, veterans might qualify for Medicaid because of their income level, but they do not apply because they feel their medical needs are being met through the Veterans Administration. However, if the senior veteran has to seek the services of a nursing home, unless it is a veterans' facility, he or she may need to apply for Medicaid if the ability to pay for nursing home care is an issue. This will include verifying a "medical necessity," as well as "spending down" to meet the qualifications for Medicaid. If this is needed, it is wise to seek the services of an attorney.

The Affordable Care Act

Since 2014, most low-income adults have been eligible for Medicaid through the Affordable Care Act. Individuals under age sixty-five with incomes below 133 percent of the Federal Poverty Level (FPL)—the minimum amount of gross income that a family needs for basic necessities—are eligible for Medicaid in every state. The Affordable Care Act refers to two separate pieces of legislation that expanded affordable Medicaid coverage to millions of low-income Americans.

Some states have what are called "medically needy" programs, which are optional for states to participate in. Individuals who have serious health problems and increasing medical needs but whose income is too high to qualify for Medicaid can still become eligible by "spending down." One way of spending down to meet that state's needy income standard is by incurring expenses for medical and remedial care. Once these expenses are incurred, they are subtracted from the person's income. If the annual income is below the state's medically needy income standard, the person may become eligible for Medicaid. In addition to medically needy programs, some states allow individuals to spend down their income to meet the state's needy income level in various other ways.[8] It is important to know your state's needy income level and if your state has spend-down programs available. Currently, there are thirty-six states and the District of Columbia that use spend-down programs.

---

[8] . "Medicaid/Medicare," www.benefits.gov (accessed June 16, 2017).

CHAPTER 6

A GUIDE TO MONITORING YOUR LOVED ONE'S HEALTH CARE AT HOME AND IN THE HOSPITAL, REHABILITATION CENTER, OR NURSING HOME

At Home

For about three years, my mother remained in her home. She had the services of two home health-care agencies, several live-in caregivers, and several housekeepers. One of the first things that one has to do when allowing someone to come into his or her house (in our case, my mother's house) is to realize that people are more important than things. Also, you have to realize that no one will take care of your loved one exactly as you would or as you would want the individual to do. However, that does not mean that you should not expect quality care for your loved one.

Once you have decided that you are going to have someone (a stranger) enter your home or your loved one's home, there are many important precautions to take in preparing your house for the caregiver's regular entry. Although you must learn to trust the people whom you employ, you should still consider storing valuable items so they do not overly attract attention. All personal information such as checkbooks, financial records, and the mail should not be readily accessible. If you are not able to collect your loved one's mail daily, I suggest that you stop mail delivery to the house and (1) either forward it to your address, or (2) obtain a post office box for future mail. In my mother's case, I chose to get a post office box.

As the senior citizen becomes more incapable of taking care of his or her business affairs, the greater the need for the responsible person to be diligent about looking for evidence of fraud, stolen IDs, and so on. If you have a landline telephone, you should start monitoring for long-distance calls. If you have cable television, start monitoring to make sure you are not paying for on-demand programs or movies that you have not authorized. It is wise to advise caregivers that they do not have the authority to make long-distance calls or to order "on demand" programming. Be suspicious of any accounts that have increased charges that you know your loved one could not have authorized. Always check statements carefully.

Being an employer or being in charge of overseeing a worker requires having some initial guidelines. The applicant should provide references, and the references should be checked out before the applicant is hired. Although most home health-care agencies will have written instructions for their workers, you still should discuss your expectations before the service begins. On the other hand, if you are privately employing someone to work for you or your loved one, you can be more specific about what your expectations and requirements are. You should begin by (1) using an application, (2) checking out the references, (3) signing a contract, and (4) making a schedule that lists exactly what the worker will be doing. Your contract should indicate what you will pay and what work will be done.

It is a good idea to have a notebook listing important information that the caregiver will need to know. Some of the items listed in the notebook should include contact information, such as emergency names and numbers, names and numbers of physicians and pharmacy, and which family members to call in case of emergency. It is also a good idea to include notes about any specific care, such as the patient's likes or dislikes (including food). My mother liked having ice cream daily. Therefore, I always made sure that ice cream was available. Caregivers also need to know about specific health problems that might not be obvious (for example, dementia or Alzheimer's disease). You will need to determine beforehand whether the individual is a private contractor or not and how Social Security and taxes will be paid.

As in all employment situations, your presence is needed as much as possible. I usually called ahead of time to let the helpers know when I would be coming and for how long. That usually gave them time to have Mother dressed (especially if we were going out) and to clean up the house. I probably should have made more drop-in, unannounced visits. I learned this after the fact. I tried to give the workers the respect of knowing that I was coming. Later I found out there were things going on in the house that I would not have approved, had I known about them. Namely, the workers were entertaining their friends and family as if they were in charge of the house. If it had been the aides from the agency, I would have needed to let the agency know. Because the workers were private contractors, I had to deal with them directly, and eventually I had to terminate two of them. The cost for maintaining the household became much more expensive because of this. The utilities, cable television, telephone, and grocery bills were higher. Therefore, it is important to stay abreast of what is going on at your house and make sure that patient care is always the priority. If it is not, you do not have the right caregiver for the job. Fortunately, my mother's house was surrounded by relatives who monitored her home as much as possible. They checked on her frequently and often saw who visited her.

Another aspect of having the patient stay in the home is taking care of the household bills, from electricity to cleaning supplies. I found that it was better for me to be the one to do the shopping for the house, but I advised the caregiver to make a list for groceries and other household items. One of the workers (Dijana) often made the list and went to the grocery store with me. She even checked the local papers for ads and knew where the best prices were. This was not a part of the job description, but she liked doing it, and I liked having her do it as well.

Finally, I emphasize that when a loved one remains at home, there are many advantages. The number one advantage is maintaining as much familiarity as possible, particularly when caring for someone who has memory loss. While at home, the individual may still be able to do some things because of the familiar locations of the rooms and familiar family faces. Having memory loss does not mean that the individual is incapable of still enjoying home, family, and friends.

In the Hospital

Once someone is admitted to the hospital, it is assumed that since the hospital has staff to monitor patients around the clock, that is what they do. Whenever it is possible, however, family members need to monitor patients—even in the hospital. In the case of my mother, she was not alert most of the time, and even when she was awake and alert, she still was not verbal. She basically responded to questions. Because I was able to stay with her at the hospital, I also was able to observe some things that would have gone unnoticed had I not been present. For example, she would not open her mouth when being fed until the spoon was on her lip. She did not respond to being told to open her mouth. Therefore, often the hospital staff would bring her meal and offer a spoonful of food, and when Mother did not open her mouth immediately, they interpreted that as "Patient refused to eat."

On several occasions, Mother was not fed. When I registered a complaint with the staff, I was repeatedly told that she would not eat. The hospital had a practice that if a patient ate slowly, the speech therapist would feed and evaluate the patient's ability to swallow. When the therapist fed her, she too recommended tubal feeding since my mother had a swallowing problem. At the time, Mother still had a good appetite and still enjoyed eating. In fact, there were few things at this point that she seemed to enjoy, and eating was one of them. At first, it seemed that I was having a problem with the aides because they refused to take the time to feed her. Then I began to notice that the nurses sometimes would not give her medicines as directed because "she refused to take it." This is when I decided that I had to do more than just monitor; I had to become actively involved in her feeding and the administering of her medicine. I had to be my mother's voice. I knew that Mother enjoyed drinking liquids, so I decided that some of her food could be given in liquid form, as well as some of her medicines. I also learned that she would eat better if she had ice cream, yogurt, applesauce, or pudding with every meal. Therefore, I requested ice cream with all of her meals, including breakfast. I fed her sometimes, but to avoid them saying that she would only eat with me, I decided to observe them feeding her most of the time. Sometimes they would feed her for a while, and I would finish.

This procedure worked okay for a short while, and then

they reverted to not feeding her adequately. At this point, it was necessary for me to register a formal complaint at the hospital. I had complained to the floor nurse earlier, and for a while I noticed improvements. Later, after my mother was totally omitted at mealtime while I was outside for a short break, I felt that I had to put an end to this situation. I read over the information regarding how to register a complaint, and I immediately contacted the director of nursing (DON). She was pleased that I had not gone to the administrator and came to her. There was a staff meeting the next day, and the DON assured me that I should see a change in my mother's care. The plan of care (POC) was that someone would be assigned to feed Mother each day, three times a day. The nurse in charge, with whom I had been very pleased, assured me that she would see to it that my mother would receive the proper care. From this point on, not only were the aides responsible for seeing that Mother was fed, but the nurses began feeding her too. As time passed, Mother continued to have a good appetite, and her feeding was no longer my primary concern. There were recurring problems with infections, low potassium, and weight loss; however, all of these improved enough that she was released from the hospital and admitted to a rehabilitation center. This transition from the hospital to the rehabilitation center gave me time to prepare mentally for the inevitable: moving her to a nursing home.

Patient Safety Tips. There are some things you need to know to be sure that your loved one receives the best care possible while in the hospital.

1. Share your loved one's health history. This includes all prescriptions, over-the-counter medications, and supplements. Also, be sure to list any allergies that the patient may have.

2. Check the identification badge. Always check for the accuracy of the information on the band. If it is not correct, have the information checked and corrected before allowing your loved one to receive any medication.

3. If you don't recognize a medication, ask the nurse what it is before the patient takes it.

4. Keep your hands clean, and ask all visitors to keep theirs clean as well. Remind those caring for your loved one to do the same if you notice they are not washing their hands, using a sanitizer, or wearing gloves.

5. If you have questions regarding the patient's condition or treatment, always ask questions.

6. Know how to take care of the patient when returning home. Make sure that a family member or a friend learns how to help with the patient at home (if going home).[9]

At the Rehabilitation Center

Before Mother left the hospital, I had been busy selecting a rehabilitation center. Mother's doctor and I had discussed two nearby facilities. Both facilities would allow her doctor to continue seeing her on a regular basis. I visited both, and because they seemed to be similar, I decided on the one that was nearest my home. I also liked the facility. This began another phase of the transition—for Mother and for me.

For the first time in over a month, I would no longer be staying with Mother around the clock. I could stay at home and sleep in my own bed now. However, I was a little concerned that I would not be able to see after Mother and make sure she was well taken care of. I knew, though, that I had to begin to trust those who

---

[9] . "Patient Safety Tips," Baylor Health Care System (a flyer I picked up at a doctor's visit).

would be taking care of her. The doctor had told me, "As long as you visit often, you will not have to worry about her care." At the facility, I had been assured that "patient care was the priority," so I tried to convince myself that I did not need to worry about her. The rehabilitation center seemed to be able to provide the care that was needed, and everyone seemed willing to make sure that the rehabilitation went well. I was assured that Medicare would continue to pay for the rehabilitation just as it had paid for the hospital stay. I was reminded of the one hundred days that Medicare and her insurance would cover for rehabilitation. I also was advised that there would be a meeting after about a week to discuss her POC while in rehab. This meeting would include nurses, therapists, the dietitian, and someone from administration. At this meeting, I could discuss any concerns I might have.

Since we were in a new place with all new staff, it was an adjustment period for all. Everyone taking care of Mother needed to be instructed on how to best care for her and how to communicate with her. At this time, she was talking even less than before. Other than an occasional reply to a question, she did not speak. The speech therapist had determined that Mother could not swallow because she ate so slowly. I did not agree, so she brought a piece of baked fish for Mother to eat to see if she could swallow it. She did not, probably because she did not like it, but it was determined that she had a swallowing problem. I had made the staff aware of her food preferences, but I had failed to let her know that Mother did not like baked fish. Thus, Mother was put on pureed food, and everything had the consistency of pudding. This was okay with me as long as she was being fed. The nurses had to learn how to give Mother her medicine in a way that she would take it with the least amount of difficulty—the best way seemed to be in a milk shake or ice cream. Just crushing the pills had not worked very well. Fortunately, it seemed that the staff appreciated my assistance and advice regarding what worked and what did not, especially when it came to feeding and to administering her pills.

After a few days in the rehabilitation center, it all started again. Mother was not being fed. The aides would simply say that she refused to eat. Of course, I knew that she would eat. One just needed to have a little patience and learn how to feed her. Just as I had done at the hospital, I had to start feeding Mother to see if she would eat—she did. The doctor had advised me that if she ate one good meal a day, that would be sufficient. She prescribed Ensure (a nutritional shake) for my mother to drink between meals, as well as with meals. So I began staying late every day until after dinner. Repeatedly, I kept hearing that she still was not eating! As she was eating almost 100 percent at dinnertime, I could not imagine that she would not eat. I had been keeping a log from the time that she was admitted to the hospital. I had always made notes of the things that needed to be discussed when the POC meeting was held. Then, one day while I was there for my daily visit, I was asked if I could come in for the family meeting on Tuesday. I agreed to come on that date. I had several written items that I had planned to discuss anyway.

On the date of the POC meeting, my husband and I met with the staff in the conference room. All were there when we arrived since they'd had an earlier meeting. The meeting started with everyone around the table introducing themselves. Afterward we were asked if we had any concerns that we would like to discuss. I began by discussing some of the things that I had on my list—mainly, the need for Mother to be fed. I had been assured that they would always have someone feed her if we chose that facility. Then I was told about the swallowing problem, and it was suggested that maybe she needed to have a feeding tube. I explained that I was no medical professional, but I would not agree to tubal feeding as long as she could still eat. I explained that when Mother had been given the baked fish to check her swallowing, she did not want to swallow because she didn't like the fish. I was again assured that I would not have to worry because as long as Mother was in that facility, she would receive the treatment needed. The dietitian said if there was anything she could do to improve the manner in which Mother was fed to let her know. I told her that at the hospital Mother received ice cream, yogurt, and applesauce at each meal—even breakfast. That usually encouraged her to eat. The dietitian said it would not be a problem to give her those items at each meal, and if she was not getting them, I should let her know. Since I knew how Mother enjoyed eating cookies (and did not seem to have a problem eating them), I said that I would continue to give her cookies and other snacks that I knew she enjoyed. I signed a waiver since it had been determined that she had a swallowing problem.

When I reported the problems that I observed with my mother's care, they seemed to be addressed, but I still questioned if this was the facility that I really wanted to take care of my mother. I had already decided that when the time came, Mother would stay at the same facility but move to the nursing home. Now I began to rethink the whole situation and ask myself, "Did I make a hasty decision?" I had to reevaluate what was going on with my mother: Are efforts being made to improve the delivery of services? Is the manner in which she is being taken care of being corrected? Will the same problems occur if she is moved? Do I really want to start over—new place, new staff, and most of all, new doctors? When I considered what was best for the patient, I still decided that we would not move Mother to another facility. I would try to see to it that she received the best possible care at this facility, and I would do my best to assist as much as possible with her care. Just as at the hospital, I had learned that the presence of a family member enhances the care that a patient receives. Therefore, I would be present.

Mother had another episode of illness and had to be hospitalized again. Because she was returned to the hospital where she originally had been admitted, it was simply a repeat of the previous visit for the most part. The main advantage was that she was returned to the wing with the same staff that had taken care of her earlier. Some staff members even seemed pleased to serve us again. We still incurred some of the same problems that happened during the first stay, but we were prepared. After another lengthy hospital stay, Mother went back to the same rehabilitation center where she had been before. I was informed that she still had forty-five Medicare days left. I had already made the decision that Mother would spend the remainder of those days in the rehabilitation center, and then she would be moved to the nursing home in the same facility. It is important to remember that my mother was no longer able to make decisions for herself. In a way, that helped me to make the decision that was inevitable—moving to a nursing home.

At the Nursing Home

Unlike the move from the hospital to the rehabilitation center, moving to the nursing home was not a big ordeal because she was simply moved to another wing in the same facility. I had been in close contact with the administrative staff and the business office. An advantage of moving to the nursing home was that she was moving to a permanent room that would now be her "home." She would have a roommate, and we were able to do some decorating to give the room some of the personal touches of home. For example, we brought the comforter from her bed and photographs of all of her children, grandchildren, and great-grandchildren. Mother was blessed to have a good roommate, Miss Addie, who had been a resident for about five years. She was still very active and was able to be another voice for Mother.

Although all of the caregivers were different from those at the rehabilitation center, the adjustment was minor. Yes, we still had many of the same challenges and complaints that we had earlier in the hospital and the rehabilitation center, but in time, Mother received the best level of care that we could expect. The one thing that must be considered wherever you choose to send your loved one is that your presence or your family's presence enhances the care of the patient. I visited daily; I visited at different times of the day, and I either fed her or witnessed her being fed almost every day. I also continued to keep a journal, and Miss Addie gave me a daily report upon my arrival.

For most of my life, I have had to deal with some serious illnesses on a personal level. Because of my parents' and my religious beliefs, I have always tried to deal with all situations from a positive standpoint. I have always relied on those beliefs when faced with dire circumstances. I believe that in learning to deal with my own health issues, it prepared me to better deal with those of my mother. She was always there for me, and I was always there for her. She had always had a positive attitude, and it was exemplified in all that she did. In sharing my personal journey in the next chapter, it will become clear how I learned to accept with joy and pride the responsibility of taking care of my mother.

CHAPTER 7

PREPARING TO BECOME A CAREGIVER

In becoming a caregiver for my mother, I had to do some serious thinking about my individual health as well. Over the years, I have experienced some serious health issues; therefore, I decided it was extremely important that I remain healthy in order to take care of my mother. The following few pages are taken from my first book, in which I describe some of the challenges that I experienced in taking care of my own health.

Living Life to the Fullest

When I was about five or six years old, I had unusually painful knee problems. For some reason, the pain always felt worse at night. Thanks to my mother and the rubbing alcohol, I was able to endure this pain without really knowing why it was occurring. All of my childhood, I can remember having this pain and resorting to the use of rubbing alcohol in order to get some relief. Actually, I think that my mother's hands were probably more soothing than the alcohol. It was difficult for me to explain the pain and probably even more difficult for my parents to understand that I had a serious problem.

In our house, we never focused on the negative things; instead, we focused on the positives. With this in mind, I learned to live with pain and to accept my limitations. Among those limitations were walking for long distances and climbing stairs. This is not to say that I did not walk for long distances—I did. This does not mean that I did not climb stairs—I did. But I did these things with difficulty. Most children did not realize that these were difficult tasks for me. I did all of the things that the other children did. However, at night I suffered from having been involved in these activities.

As I grew into my teens, I noticed that most of the other young girls could do a few exercises that I could not do. I had problems touching my toes. At the time, I was a trim, seemingly healthy young lady, but I could not touch my toes. However, I was good at playing basketball; I was a good shot, and I had a good high kick when exercising in physical education classes. Therefore, touching my toes was not a real concern—I just knew that I could not. After all, young ladies don't bend to pick up things from the floor; they squat or kneel.

I first suspected that I had arthritis when I was about sixteen or seventeen. My mother took me to the doctor (Dr. Lane) in Wills Point. At the time, he was probably the most popular doctor for African Americans in Emory. He did not give me a diagnosis of arthritis, but he gave me arthritis medicine. I thought that it was somewhat ironic that I was taking the same medication as one of my aunts (Aunt Gletha), who also was taking it for arthritis. I continued taking this medication on and off throughout college. Sometimes I would think that the illness was gone, and then something would happen to let me know that it was still present. For example, once I was walking across the college campus while at East Texas State and it was raining. I had my umbrella up, and I was well protected from the rain. However, as I was walking, suddenly my legs just completely failed to move. I could go no farther! I stood there holding my umbrella for what seemed like minutes (even though it was probably only a few seconds) until my legs would continue moving.

There were similar instances when my legs just seemed to refuse to move. Occasionally, when climbing stairs, I would get to the top but could not go any farther. Or I would start down and not be able to make it to the bottom of the stairs. Fortunately, whenever this happened, it would only be for a short period. But for the most part, I always seemed quite healthy otherwise. Then, after not having problems for a while, I decided to stop taking the medication.

Upon moving to Dallas and being hired by the Dallas Independent School District, I had to have a physical examination. At the recommendation of a friend, I went to Dr. Mason, an African American doctor on Forest Avenue in South Dallas (which is where most African American doctors were at that time). He was one of the most noted doctors in the community. I vividly remember going to Dr. Mason and having a blood test. I was told that "sugar" (diabetes) showed up in the test. Since I had eaten before the test and had a soft drink with my lunch, he suggested that I come back on the following day before eating. I can remember that being a "very long" evening—wondering whether or not I was diabetic.

As a lover of desserts, all I could think about was the banana pudding that I was planning to make (from scratch) that evening. I could not imagine being unable to eat all of the desserts and breads that I had always loved so much.

When I returned to Dr. Mason's office the next day for my blood test, much to my surprise and pleasure, I found out that what I had was "low" blood sugar. He said that it was just a little low and would need to be monitored. Therefore, I had nothing to be worried about.

Since I had gone to Dr. Mason for my initial examination for the Dallas Independent School District, I decided that he would be my primary physician. I didn't know of any others anyway. For several years, when I had colds, flu, aches, pains, etc., I always went to him. It was Dr. Mason who finally told me that I did have arthritis. So, once again, I began taking medications.

Once when I was ill, I went to another doctor because he was closer and I was driving myself. I had not taken the arthritis medication for a while. I was having stomach cramps and was very sick. He was concerned that I had stopped taking my medication. I told him that I had not been bothered with arthritis lately. He explained, "There is no cure for arthritis," and that I should continue taking the medication. He said by not taking my medication, I had probably made myself sick. I asked him, "How long do I need to be on medication?" He said, "As long as you live." At this point, I could not believe that I would have to take any medication for the rest of my life—not for arthritis. I kept thinking, "I'm young; I'm only in my twenties!" I decided that it was time that I started to read more about my illness and my medications.

A few years passed, and I only had minor arthritis problems. One day, while running a few errands, I decided to stop at a nearby Wyatt's Cafeteria in the Wynnewood Shopping Center. I can remember having minor difficulty walking inside. Once inside, I could not walk any farther. My legs seemed to have frozen; I could not move. This was very frightening. Somehow, with the assistance of my daughter, I was able to make it back to my car. It was at this point I decided that I had to know what was going on with my body— and my legs! At this time, Dr. Mason was no longer my physician … I had started going to a general practitioner at St. Paul Hospital by the name of Dr. Woodard. I called Dr. Woodard that afternoon and made an appointment for the next day.

After many tests, Dr. Woodard explained to me that a very rare form of arthritis had shown up in my blood test. The rare disease was called lupus. He said that I should not be too concerned and that he would order more tests. After taking more tests, I was pleased to hear that the lupus did not show up. However, a short time after that, I was sick again and unable to walk. I thought it was the arthritis. I knew that arthritis affected all of my joints, so I took some time off from work hoping that my legs would get better and that I would not be ill anymore. Unfortunately, that did not happen. Not only did my legs hurt, but I was also very sick.

Once again I was back in Dr. Woodard's office trying to find out what was wrong with me. He ordered more tests. After getting the test results, Dr. Woodward said there was a specialist, Dr. Stanley Cohen, whom he would like me to see. However, Dr. Cohen was very expensive and I might not want to see him because of the cost. Although I respected Dr. Woodard, I was offended that he assumed I would not want to seek the help of a specialist because it was expensive. Even though my funds were somewhat scarce, I assured him that I would like the referral. I felt he might have assumed that because I was African American, I could not afford Dr. Cohen.

When I entered Dr. Cohen's office, I was somewhat apprehensive. I had been upset with Dr. Woodard for telling me that he would be expensive, but now I was wondering just how expensive he would be. When I had gone to the other doctors for my arthritis problems, the first thing I had to do was have blood drawn. This time it was different. Dr. Cohen came in and introduced himself. Except for the fact that he looked my age—I had imagined a specialist should be older—I was very impressed. For the first time, I met a doctor who seemed to be genuinely interested in my illness and in me. He sat down and described to me what lupus is and whom it usually affects (young African American women), and said I should be able to live with the illness. It was not very encouraging, however. I learned that prior to the 1950s, most women suffering with lupus died in their thirties. At this point, I felt that maybe my future was not so bright! But with the knowledge I gained from Dr. Cohen and from reading about the disease, I decided that I would just live life to the fullest! My disease would not keep me from doing the things that I enjoyed most.

I thought that one of the best ways to not be affected by having lupus would be to not let anyone know that I had it—except for the few people closest to me.

Before this writing, I had let this remain "my illness," and I had not burdened others (even family and friends) with my complaints. This had often been very hard because of all the illnesses I have endured that related to having lupus. I also had been taking lots of medications, and often they were (in my opinion) just as bad as being sick. In fact, sometimes I have taken medication to prevent the other medications from making me sick. I have even had to start going to an ophthalmologist on a regular basis because lupus medication can cause color blindness.

If having a disease that usually ends up in death was not enough, you might say that I have also received what could be labeled as a second "death sentence." This all started with a cough that I could not stop. For several years, I went to Dr. Cohen, as well as other primary care physicians (PCPs), in an effort to find out why I could not stop coughing. Because I have lupus, it was thought that maybe it was connected to the disease. Therefore, I was sent to several specialists—ear, nose, and throat specialists; lung specialists; etc. I also have had all kinds of tests (X-rays, swallowing tests, CT scans of my lungs and sinuses, etc.) to try to determine the cause of the cough. However, no real conclusion was made. The doctors just said that I had a respiratory problem or infection.

For several years, I had complained that I thought the air quality in my classroom was unsafe. I noticed that whenever school was in session, I always had problems with coughing. Whenever school was not in session, my breathing was better. Asbestos had been cited as the cause of illness for a number of workers in the school district over the years. I thought that perhaps the asbestos had affected me. But more than being concerned about asbestos, I was concerned that the air I was breathing in my classroom was not safe. At one time, the temperature in my classroom was averaging about 95 degrees, and this was in January and February, often when there was ice on the ground outside. I complained to the principal, the custodian, and basically anyone who would listen.

Finally, I filed a grievance with the school district because I felt that this classroom was unsafe. Someone from environmental services came out and tested the air quality (and temperature). The ducts were cleaned and an air-conditioning unit was placed in the classroom to circulate the air during the winter months. This did help my breathing, but I cannot say that this was the solution. After a few more years of teaching in that classroom, and registering a number of additional complaints, I was moved to the classroom across the hall. It was a bigger room, and the circulation was a little better. However, no one ever gave me copies of any of the tests that were performed to determine the air quality as I had been promised. I just know that there were times that breathing was very hard.

From this point on, I had to be extremely careful whenever I had any kind of respiratory problem. And it was not long before I did have another incidence of sickness. This time I was at home alone in the middle of winter. It was very cold, and I was very sick. I considered calling an ambulance, but I decided that I was well enough to drive myself— big mistake! When I got to the doctor's office, I was too sick to sit up in the waiting room. After a short while, I was taken in to see a doctor (Dr. Waymon Drummond) at St. Paul Hospital. He in turn had the nurses get a wheelchair, and he sent me to be admitted. After being admitted for pneumonia and undergoing numerous tests, several specialists seemed to agree that my lungs had been extensively damaged. The first question that each one asked was "How long have you smoked?" They would not ask *if* I smoked but *how long*? Dr. Cohen seemed to have a better understanding of my illness and how to treat me for it. Until now he had been my rheumatologist, but I considered him my main doctor.

After having another serious bout of coughing, I went to the doctor and was given medication. Because I was really ill, he gave me some samples and a prescription. When I got home, I took the medication and had the prescription filled. In less than an hour, I had to call 911 and was rushed to the hospital. Once again, I was admitted to St. Paul Hospital. This time Dr. Drummond told me if I had not made it to the hospital when I did, I would probably have died. I was that near death! I had taken a medication that I was allergic to. It would seem that after all of the medications I had taken, someone would have known of my allergy—even though I did not!

After I survived the latest coughing bout and the reaction to the medication, I was referred to a pulmonary (lung) and asthma specialist, Dr. Pedro Zevallos. Dr. Zevallos began treating me for my lung disease. After frequent X-rays, CT scans, blood tests, etc., it was determined that my lungs were damaged (scarred) beyond repair. This was the first time that I had actually been told that there was no cure and no way to repair my lungs. I was also told that this damage was not related to having lupus. Since the doctors had no way of determining when the scarring took place (or why), I would need to learn how to deal with two life-threatening conditions: lupus and lung disease.

Since there was no cure for either of them, I had to learn to live with the diseases and to live life to the fullest! One of the ways that the doctor suggested was to take therapy (pulmonary and physical). He even suggested that at some point I might be a candidate for a lung transplant. Since I have already lived far beyond the normal life expectancy of an individual with lupus and I have lived a number years with lung disease, I am convinced that I am handling my diseases and not letting them handle me! My plans are to just keep on defying the odds and—living life to the fullest![10]

Because I have always tried to look at aging in a positive light, it is only natural that I have accepted my mother's situation as inspiration for me to continue to accept what is and reflect positively on what was. My mother and I had an opportunity to establish a new relationship. I looked forward to seeing her every day, and I liked thinking that the feeling was mutual. Over the years, I saw her health deteriorate to the extent that she did not speak most of the time that I spent with her. On the other hand, there were days that she smiled when she saw me or heard my voice. I continued learning to live my life to the fullest and to see to it that she was able to do the same. I treasured every moment that we spent together. I knew that there were changes in the relationship, but I prayed that I would continue to have the strength to be with her during this age of transition.

The best way that you can prepare to be a caregiver is to first learn how to take care of yourself. Once you become the caregiver of a loved one, you have to be physically and mentally up to the challenge; and that starts by being in charge of your own health care. Otherwise, how will you be able to take care of someone if you are not healthy? There is a saying, "The young man takes care of the old man." There is a lot of truth in this statement. It literally means that if you take care of yourself as a young person, you will be healthier as an old person. (Or it could mean that if you do

---

[10] . Gwendolyn McMillan Lawe, *From Wolf to Wolfwood* (Bloomington, IN: AuthorHouse, 2011), 135–143.

not take care of yourself, you may not live to be an old person!) Therefore, it is wise to take care of yourself first.

Taking care of you starts with getting plenty of rest, eating healthy foods, getting plenty of exercise, and having a preventive health program. For example, be sure that you take regular preventive measures, such as flu and pneumonia shots, and mammograms or prostate screenings, as suggested by a physician. If you are diabetic or have a preexisting condition that you are aware of and are being treated for, be sure to follow the plan of care that your doctor has prescribed for you. Have regular checkups, including dental and vision.

An important part of being a caregiver includes taking time off to take care of you. It is important to take breaks, particularly if you are giving care on a daily basis. Sometimes you might need a day; at other times, you might need to take as long as a week. A vacation—however short—might be just what you need in order to maintain your health (physical and mental).

Also, when you become a caregiver, you learn a lot about getting your own business affairs in order. This includes evaluating your finances (making sure that you have someone named on your accounts upon your death) and insurance (life and health), and being sure that you have the proper documentation for the time when you can no longer take care of yourself. Be sure that you have made arrangements for the end of your life—i.e., a will, power of attorney, etc.—and make sure that someone near you knows the location of all of your necessary documents. If you have an attorney, it is important that someone has that information as well.

If, as a caregiver, you have experienced working with home health-care agencies, hospitals, rehabilitation centers, and nursing homes, you might have a definite idea about where you one day want to (or do not want to) receive care for yourself. After visiting several facilities, you might have become familiar with what they offer and how they meet your particular interests and needs.

Finally, make sure that someone knows your final wishes. Although most people do not want to discuss their final wishes, someone needs to know what they are. For example, do you want to be cremated or do you want to be buried? Do you have a prepaid funeral policy? Do you want a traditional funeral or just a memorial service? Remember, if you never express your wishes, it will be up to someone else to carry out his or her wishes instead.

CHAPTER 8

FROM THE NURSING HOME TO THE HOSPITAL

(Back and Forth)

One of the most difficult times when caring for a loved one is returning to the hospital from the nursing home—usually through the emergency room. Once your loved one reaches the final stage of life, it seems that the visits to the hospital become more frequent. Each time I received the call that my mother was being taken to the hospital, I began praying for the best and, at the same time, preparing for the worst. It was also at this time that I started to evaluate just what "the best" and "the worst" really were. I always tried not to be selfish (which is virtually impossible) and to look at the situation in terms of what was the best for the patient—not for me.

You reach a point where some serious decisions have to be made. For example, what is the expected outcome of various procedures (such as surgery) if they are performed at this point in life? What are the chances of survival? Are the survival chances worth the risks? If the patient has an advance directive, it would not be up to the responsible person to make such decisions. Unfortunately, in my case (which is the most common situation), there was no advance directive. Therefore, I had to make many decisions based on what I thought would be best for my mother. If the decisions had to be made immediately, I made the decisions myself. However, if there were situations that I needed to think about before giving an answer, I usually consulted with my brother, my husband, and sometimes other family members.

One of the hardest things at this stage is convincing yourself that you are doing the right thing. Doctors, nurses, and others will start to question your feelings about hospice care and palliative care. This is usually a reminder that the end is near. However, approximately two years ago, the doctor in my mother's hometown recommended that I consider hospice. At that time, she was still living at home and maintaining a reasonably functional lifestyle with the assistance of a caregiver and the services of a home health agency. I did not do an in-depth check into his motivations, but I later heard that he was part owner of a hospice service. That would explain why he might recommend hospice to someone who was still enjoying life at home and not needing end-of-life care.

In doing my research on hospice care, my brother and I decided that we would not place our mother in hospice. Although I feel this is a worthwhile service, I was neither ready nor willing to place my mother in hospice at the time. However, just as it is true with most patients who have some form of dementia, the disease doesn't get better. Therefore, as time passed, the Alzheimer's began to cause my mother's condition to decline rapidly. She was in and out of the hospital more frequently. During most of the time that she spent in the nursing home and the hospital, she did not seem to be experiencing much pain, but she reached a point when she was not feeling well and was not responding to me as she had done in the past. She was not eating well, and consequently she was beginning to lose weight. As before, I stayed at her bedside and tried to assist in her care as much as I could.

Upon her last return to the nursing home, after several days' stay in the hospital because of an infection, an irregular heart rate, and some other difficulties, I decided it was time to consider palliative care. Unlike being in hospice, she would still be on her medications and treatments, but she would not be taken to the hospital again. I felt that her body was weak and that she should not be subjected to the hospital anymore. In talking with her physician, as well as the facility staff, it was decided that she would not return to the hospital and that the caregivers at the nursing home would do their best to keep her comfortable during her final days. It was then that I agreed to and signed the DNR (do not resuscitate) papers.

I continued my daily visits, but it was clear to me that my mother was slowly making her final transition. I still held her hand, and she held mine. However, I could tell that she was losing her grip. Previously when I visited, she would hold my hand and let me know that she did not want me to leave. Some days, she slept the entire time I was there. I had learned that if she was sleeping quietly, she was resting and was not in pain.

In December, I began spending more time with my mother. I had always gone to visit on a daily basis, but now I knew that soon I would not be able to visit at all. I conveyed this to my brothers, my daughter, other extended family members, and my close friends. The support of family and friends is always so important to the caregiver at this time. Fortunately, I had lots of support. Although I don't know if she was aware of it, my mother had frequent visits from her grandchildren, great-grandchildren, nieces and nephews, and friends, as well as her immediate family members.

On the evening of my last visit, Mother exhibited pain—more than in the past. She was having complications; she was not eating, and she was very, very weak. I stayed longer and felt I should stay as long as possible. I was not aware that this would be my final visit.

On the morning of December 12, 2014 (one day before her eighty-ninth birthday), I received a call from the nursing facility that my mother, Modis Robinson McMillan, had made her final transition. Although the news was sad, I was comforted in knowing that all of her suffering was over. She was at peace, and so was I.

CHAPTER 9

BEING CAREGIVER TO A SPOUSE

(An Unintended Chapter)

In 2011, I retired. I realized that I would have to spend more time seeing to it that my mother received the types of care that she needed. At the time, she was still living alone and only needed a little care. She was still able to perform her day-to-day activities, and she was still able to drive her car. She did realize that she was beginning to need some assistance with her financial and other business transactions. This was understandable. She was in her eighties.

I recently was faced with a totally new experience: I became my spouse's caregiver. After my mother's death, my husband expressed that he hoped if he were to become ill, he would not have a lengthy illness. He said he knew that I was a caregiver, and he did not want me to have to care for him for an extended period. I teased him and said, "You don't have any choice about the length of your illness or how you will die!"

During the last year of my mother's life, because I had tried to spend time with her daily, my husband and I did not get to travel as much as we had over the previous years. We began making plans for a two-week road trip, which was what we had done each year for several years. We decided to attend a conference, visit relatives and friends, and take in some cultural and historical sites as a part of our summer vacation. Unfortunately, after making these plans (which included getting hotel reservations, registering for a national conference, and reserving a rental car), Ted learned that he had a serious problem with anemia and he should not take the two-week road trip. Needless to say, we were both disappointed, but we knew that he needed to take his doctor's advice. Therefore, since his referral to see a hematologist was a week away, Ted suggested that we take a shorter trip—a weekend vacation—which we did. He was overly apologetic, but I explained to him that we would accept and get through whatever the diagnosis was.

After taking our trip, we went to the scheduled appointment with the hematologist and made a second appointment for some outpatient tests. When we went for the MRI, there was a problem with the machine and the test was rescheduled for later in the week. (This made us think that perhaps the test was not urgent.) A couple of days later, Ted was not feeling well, and he was having some breathing difficulties. I convinced him that we should call the paramedics. We called and he was taken to the hospital. He spent the night and was released the next afternoon. I really thought that he should not have been released, but the doctors said they saw no reason for him to be kept in the hospital. We went home.

Two days later, when I took Ted to the hematologist's office, Ted was so weak that I had to use a wheelchair when we arrived. Seeing how weak he was, the doctor called the hospital and requested that his primary doctor do a direct admission. I took him to the hospital, and he was admitted. While there, after a complete evaluation, they did the test that he previously had been scheduled to take. After a day and one overnight, his doctor stated that Ted should only be there a couple of days. However, a couple of days turned into a little more than a week. Each day his prognosis was worse. What started as a short visit for tests and evaluation became my husband's final days of his life. As with my mother, I stayed with him in the hospital around the clock.

At first, I had no idea that I was spending time with him as he made his final transition. Because he was alert and aware of his surroundings, we talked, we held hands, and I prayed and played music for him. But after the second day, it became apparent that Ted was not getting better; he was getting worse daily (maybe hourly). I decided that it was time for me to call immediate family members and my best friends. Ted had previously asked that I would not notify anyone of his illness. He said by the time I let them know, he would be home. However, once we knew that he would not be home soon, I called the family. Both children, two of his grandsons, and his only sister came to visit. He was aware of their visits and was glad to see them. He was glad that I had gone against his wishes and called them.

Although I was not really ready to be caring for my husband in his last days, I was better prepared because I had been my mother's caregiver. I knew a lot about what I had to do. I knew that I had to be by his side and give him as much of my attention as I could give. I told him how much I loved him; he told me how much he loved me. I assured him that I would be there until the end, and he knew I would. As time passed, his speech became unclear and he was heavily medicated. However, I continued to talk to him even if he did not or could not answer. I had done the same thing for my mother. I continued to play music for him as I had done for my mother. As he was making his final transition, I played our wedding song, "You Needed Me" by Ann Murray, several times. I asked him if he recognized it, and he said, "It's our song." At this time, we needed each other.

GLOSSARY

When caring for an elder person, there are some Medicare definitions that the caregiver needs to know. These terms are described in more detail in the *Medicare & You 2018* publication.

Benefit period—Original Medicare measures the use of hospital and skilled nursing facility (SNF) services beginning the day the individual is admitted as an inpatient. The benefit period ends when the patient has not received inpatient care for sixty consecutive days.

Coinsurance—This refers to the amount that the patient may be required to pay for services after paying for any deductibles.

Copayment—This is the amount that the patient may be required to pay as a share of the cost for medical services, such as a hospital outpatient visit or prescriptions.

Critical access hospital—In rural communities, a facility that provides outpatient and inpatient services on a limited basis is called a critical access hospital.

Custodial care—Help with such nonskilled personal care activities as bathing, dressing, eating, and getting in and out of bed is referred to as custodial care. Medicare usually does not pay for this type of care.

Inpatient rehabilitation facility—This facility (hospital or part of a hospital) provides inpatients with an intensive rehabilitation program.

Institution—Based on Medicare's definition, this is a facility that provides either short-term or long-term care, such as a nursing home, skilled nursing facility (SNF), or rehabilitation hospital. Assisted living facilities or group homes are not considered institutions for Medicare purposes.

Lifetime reserve days—This term refers to the additional days that Medicare will pay for when a patient is in the hospital for more than ninety days. The patient has a total of sixty reserve days that may be used during his or her lifetime.

Long-term care—Medicare and most insurance plans do not pay for long-term care. These services include medical and nonmedical care for people who are unable to perform basic daily living activities (dressing, bathing, etc.).

Long-term care hospital—An acute care hospital that provides treatment, on average, for more than twenty-five days is called a long-term care hospital. Services provided at this type of institution include comprehensive rehabilitation as well as other therapies and treatments.

Premium—This is a periodic payment made to Medicare, an insurance company, or a health-care plan for health care or prescription drug coverage.

Preventive services—Health care to prevent illness or to detect an illness at an early stage is called preventive services. This includes such services as pap tests, mammograms, and flu shots.

Primary care doctor—This is the doctor who is seen first for most health problems.

Referral—A written order from the primary care doctor to see a specialist or to get certain medical services is a referral.

Skilled nursing facility (SNF) care—This refers to skilled nursing and rehabilitation services provided on a continuous basis by skilled nursing personnel. A skilled nursing facility is often referred to as a nursing home or a rehabilitation center.[11]

---

[11] . "Section 11: Definitions," *Medicare & You,* Center for Medicare & Medicaid Services (2018), 129–132.

APPENDIX A

Helpful Websites for Senior Health Resources

1. National Association of Area Agencies on Aging, www.n4a.org
2. Area Agency on Aging of Dallas, www.ccgd.org
3. New Lifestyles, www.newlifestyles.com
4. Administration on Aging, www.aoa.gov
5. Texas Department of Aging and Disability Services, www.dads.state.tx.us/contact\aaa.cfm
6. VNA Aging Resources—federal, state, local, nonprofit, www.vnatexas.org
7. Senior Source-Dallas, www.theseniorsource.org
8. Senior Agencies, www.ask.com/senior+agencies
9. Free Senior Assistance, www.elderhelpers.org
10. Texas Seniors' Guides, www.seniorsguide.net
11. Senior Citizens' Resources—USA.gov, www.usa.gov/topics/seniors
12. Senior Care Resource Links, www.seniorhelpers.com/Resourcelinks
13. Medicaid, www.medicaid.gov
14. Medicare, www.medicare.gov
15. National Senior Citizen Law Center, www.nsclc.org
16. Federal websites—Eldercare Locator, www.eldercare.gov/eldercare.net/public/

17. Senior communities in Texas—pricing, ratings, and reviews for over 105,000 communities, www.senioradvisor.com
18. Resources for seniors, www.aarp.com
19. *Seniorific News,* Serving Seniors and Caregivers with Information to Improve the Best Time of Life ... Today, www.seniorific.com/epub
20. The Alzheimer's Association, incorporated in 1980 as Alzheimer's Disease and Other Related Disorders Association, Inc., www.alz.org

APPENDIX B

A Beautiful Life

Because I was inspired to write this book after caring for my mother and becoming aware of all of the things one needs to know when caring for the elderly or disabled, I thought it was also necessary to write about this beautiful person—my mother.

An Obituary

Modis Robinson McMillan

December 13, 1925—December 12, 2014

Modis Robinson McMillan

On December 13, 1925, Modis Robinson McMillan was born in Emory, Texas. She was the youngest of nine children (four sisters and four brothers) born to Henry Robinson and Lucy Bridges Robinson. A lifetime resident of Emory, Texas, Modis grew up living with her parents, her grandfather (Sampson "Pete" Bridges), and her siblings (Elma, Virgie, Loda, Gletha, Lonnie, Ozell, Lorenza, and Choycie). Elma married E. Hobbs of Point, Virgie married Orie Potter of Greenville, Lonnie married Mattie Lee Phillips, Loda married Harvey Kendrick, Gletha married Albert Davis, Ozell married Annie Woosley, Lorenza married Nina Johnson, and Choycie married Doris Robinson of Winnsboro. He later moved to Los Angeles, California.

As Modis was quite younger than her oldest siblings, she still lived at home with her parents after her siblings married and moved away. Virgie and Loda were the only sisters to move out of town and out of state when they married. Virgie moved to Greenville, Texas, and Loda moved to Venice, California. Virgie and her husband, Orie, traveled a lot (for people during that time). Modis often visited with them and also traveled with them to Los Angeles to visit Loda and her family. Virgie purchased a home and moved back to Emory after the death of her husband and later lived with Modis until her (Virgie's) death. Their brother, Choycie, also moved back to Emory. He lived with Modis for a while but was in a nursing home in Sulphur Springs at the time of his death.

Modis attended Sand Flat School. At that time, Sand Flat was the only school for African Americans and only went through tenth grade. On November 16, 1941, Modis married A. C. McMillan. During their marriage, they briefly lived in Durham, North Carolina, while he was serving in the United States Army. They lived in Tyler, Texas, while A. C. attended Texas College. When he graduated in 1949, he became the principal at Sand Flat School in Emory. From that time on, they lived in Emory.

Modis and A. C. were parents to four children, Alfred, Jewel, Gwendolyn, and Harold. For most of her life, Modis was a housewife who was always available to support her husband in his work and their children in their many school activities. After her children grew up and moved away from home, Modis decided to continue her education and earn the high school diploma she had not been able to receive because Sand Flat only went to the tenth grade. Through the efforts of her husband, adult basic education classes were offered in Emory at the Sand Flat School building. This gave several other individuals in the community an opportunity to earn their GEDs as well. It was a proud moment in the lives of all who took the classes when they received their GEDs.

During her husband's lifetime, Modis and A. C. were pillars of the community. He was a teacher and principal, a Sunday school superintendent, and a trustee at the church. They did lots of community work together, but most memorable was their love of children. The couple allowed numerous children to live in their home when they were having problems at their own homes and needed a place to stay for a while—a night, a week, or more. At other times, several nieces (great and great-great) and granddaughters also stayed with them for a few months and even years. After the death of Modis's husband, one of her nephews, Willie Mornes, volunteered to stay with her so she would not be alone. That was the beginning of a special bond between the two. He stayed with her at night until she felt comfortable being alone. Years later, when she could no longer live alone and a niece needed a place to stay, she again opened her doors. Her doors were always open.

Since the school and the church were the centers for community activities, Modis spent a lot of time attending various programs at the school. Later, after desegregation, A. C. became the junior high principal at Rains (previously the white school). Their children were no longer in school at Sand Flat, so Modis became equally involved in the activities and programs at Rains. She worked briefly for NET Opportunities at the senior center and participated in such classes as cooking, quilting, and ceramics as part of the senior programs. The senior center was located in the Sand Flat School building.

Modis remained married until the death of her husband in 1986. The A. C. McMillan Scholarship, named in his honor, was awarded by the McMillan family to a deserving student at Rains High School in 1987. Modis served as president of the scholarship fund. To date, approximately fifty scholarships have been given.

A lifetime member of the Prairie Grove Baptist Church, Modis sang in the choir, worked with the youth, and was a church clerk, deaconess, and mission president. She was a member of the Heroines of Jericho. She was active in the Cypress District Association in the Sunday school and mission departments. She often attended the Fifth Sunday board meetings, the association meetings, and the annual Baptist Sunday School and BTU (Baptist Training Union) Congress. The Cypress meetings were some of the most memorable in Prairie Grove Baptist Church's history.

Some of the civic organizations in which she was involved included the Rains County Genealogical Society, the Women's Service Club, the Rains County Garden Club, and the Economic Development Corporation. Although she did not use the computer, Modis found joy in hearing about her ancestors through information obtained from US Census records on the Internet. She often reminisced about her maternal grandfather, Pete Bridges, and she learned more about him through reading the material found on the Internet.

At the age of seventy-four, Modis began a new career. She became the coordinator of volunteer services for the A. C. McMillan African American Museum, which was founded in 2000 in memory of her husband. This started a new chapter of her life. She, along with several other volunteers (Florene McMillan, Clarissa McMillan, Mildred Garrett, Addine Thomas, Audie Mae Shiflet, Esta Mae Peeples, Annie Ruth Pickrom, Modean Lane, and Fannon and Dave Garrett), began what would be thirteen years of museum life. Through her involvement in the museum, she attended meetings of the Texas Association of Museums (Lubbock), the East Texas Historical Association (Waco), and several other regional meetings. She and the volunteers served as hosts for receptions, tour groups, day camps, school field trips, and many other museum programs. In 2013, due to her failing health, Modis was no longer able to keep up her activities at the museum.

Of all of her lifelong responsibilities, her favorite titles were wife, mother, grandmother, and aunt. Nothing made her prouder than entertaining her children, her son-in-law, her grandchildren, her great-grandchildren, and anyone who might come for dinner on a holiday, such as Easter, Mother's Day, Thanksgiving, or Christmas. The holiday meal was basically the same on each of these days. She particularly enjoyed family reunions and holiday gatherings. During her later years, Modis and her family joined with Florene McMillan's family to celebrate the holidays. These get-togethers were enjoyed by all and enabled each participant to be responsible for only certain items instead of the whole meal. Their daughters, Gwendolyn and Dianne, were especially fond of combining the event. Otherwise, they would have been charged with the responsibility of trying to duplicate what their mothers had always done—cooking big meals!

In November 2013, Modis McMillan entered the hospital in Mesquite, Texas. After spending several weeks there, she moved to a rehabilitation facility for several months before entering a nursing home in Mesquite to be near her only daughter, Gwendolyn.

Modis's children are Alfred C. McMillan, Jr., of Emory; Gwendolyn McMillan Lawe (married to Theodore M. Lawe), Dallas; and Harold McMillan, Austin. Another son, Jewel "Chief" McMillan, lived in Lake Jackson when he passed in 2012. Her grandchildren are Yolanda Edwards, Dallas; April McMillan, Dallas; Stacye Hargrove, Cypress; Sylvia Lawe Williams, Longview; and Hayes McMillan, Austin. Her great-grandchildren are Mechelle Edwards, Mitchell Edwards, Taylor McMillan, Timothy McMillan, Preston Lawe, Blair Williams, Sydney Hargrove, Aaron Hargrove, and William Hargrove. Mitchell Edwards III is her only great-great-grandson.

Modis's later life was spent at the Willow Bend Nursing and Rehabilitation Center in Mesquite, Texas. There, she and her daughter spent every afternoon together enjoying each other—living life to the fullest!

Modis's husband (A. C.) and one son, Jewel, preceded her in death, as well as all of her siblings. Most of her childhood and lifelong friends preceded her in death as well. They included childhood friends Ida Beth Collins and Ponsella Boyce, and lifelong adult friends Deora McMillan Garrett, Alene Nash Randolph, Bonnie Willie Williams, Clarissa Cooks McMillan, Modis Turner Mayberry, and Florene Blaylock McMillan.

Modis Robinson McMillan died on December 12, 2014, in Mesquite, Texas. Modis Robinson McMillan—her beautiful smile, her soft-spoken voice, and her loving personality—is greatly missed by many.

ABOUT THE AUTHOR

Gwendolyn McMillan Lawe is also the author of *From Wolf to Wolfwood*, and she has written many articles on various topics. She was born in Emory, Texas. After graduating from Rains High School, she attended and graduated from Henderson County Junior College (now Trinity Valley Community College). She continued her education at East Texas State University (now Texas A&M University-Commerce) where she received a bachelor's degree in business education and a master's degree in guidance.

Following in her father's footsteps, Gwendolyn became a teacher in the Dallas Independent School District, where she retired in 2011. Teaching was paramount in the writer's professional career; however, she also cofounded and served as director of College Bound Tours. In addition, she is cofounder of the A. C. McMillan Scholarship Fund (in memory of her father), which annually awards scholarships at Rains High School, and cofounder of the A. C. McMillan African American Museum, where she serves as its director.

Her organizational affiliations include Alpha Kappa Alpha Sorority, the Dallas Theater Center Guild, the African American Museum, New Hope Baptist Church, American Baptist Women, South Dallas Business and Professional Women's Club, the Rains County Genealogical Association, the East Texas Historical

Association, and the National Trust for Historic Preservation. Her volunteer work with these organizations and others is extensive.

Her awards and recognitions include winner of the NAACP Juanita Craft Award for Community Service, the Elks Award for Community Service, and Outstanding Ex-Student/Trinity Valley Community College. In 2000, she won the "Women of Wonder," a national award for community service presented by the Quaker Oats Company. She received a Visiting Professional Fellowship from the prestigious Smithsonian Institution and studied at the Smithsonian in Washington, DC, during the summer of 2003. In 2004 and 2005, she was awarded scholarships to attend the National Trust for Historic Preservation conferences in Louisville, Kentucky, and Portland, Oregon, respectively. She was recognized in 2007 as a role model by the Epsilon Sigma Chapter of Alpha Kappa Alpha Sorority at Texas A&M University-Commerce, and in 2010 by the South Dallas Business and Professional Women's Club during Women's History Month (March). In 2016, she was recognized with the "We Speak Your Name" award at the South Central District's 54th Annual Conference in Addison, Texas.

Gwendolyn McMillan Lawe is a retired business education teacher. She lives in Dallas, Texas, where she continues to be active in many civic organizations. She has a daughter, Sylvia Lawe Williams, and two grandsons, Preston Lawe and Blair Williams.

Printed in the United States
By Bookmasters